THE FIRST BOOK OF BAHA'I PRAYERS

The First Book of Baha'i Prayers

PRAYERS REVEALED BY BAHA'U'LLAH, THE BAB, AND 'ABDU'L-BAHA

An original "Stone with Seven Eyes" publication.

BAHA'I PUBLISHERS
UNDER THE PROVISIONS OF THE COVENANT
MISSOULA, MONTANA

FIRST EDITION, 1900.
ENLARGED, 1969.
EXPANDED, 2013.

ISBN: 0-9767389-9-6

www.UHJ.net
www.BUPC.org

Intone, O My servants, the verses of God that have been received by thee, as intoned by them who have drawn nigh unto Him, that the sweetness of thy melody may kindle thine own soul, and attract the hearts of all men. Whoso reciteth, in the privacy of his chamber, the verses revealed by God, the scattering angels of the Almighty shall scatter abroad the fragrance of the words uttered by his mouth, and shall cause the heart of every righteous man to throb. Though he may, at first, remain unaware of its effect, yet the virtue of the grace vouchsafed unto him must needs sooner or later exercise its influence upon his soul. Thus have the mysteries of the Revelation of God been decreed by virtue of the will of Him Who is the Source of power and wisdom.

- Baha'u'llah -

TABLE OF CONTENTS

PRAISE AND GRATITUDE

PRAYER FOR AMERICA

PROTECTION

SEVERANCE

SPIRITUAL QUALITIES

BAHA'I PRAYERS
FOR GENERAL USE

ASSISTANCE

A

My God, my Adored One, my King, my Desire! What tongue can voice my thanks to Thee? I was heedless, Thou didst awaken me. I had turned back from Thee, Thou didst graciously aid me to turn toward Thee. I was as one dead, Thou didst quicken me with the water of life. I was withered, Thou didst revive me with the heavenly stream of Thine utterance which hath flowed forth from the Pen of the All-Merciful.

O Divine Providence! All existence is begotten by Thy bounty; deprive it not of the waters of Thy generosity, neither do Thou withhold it from the ocean of Thy mercy. I beseech Thee to aid and assist me at all times and under all conditions, and seek from the heaven of Thy grace Thine ancient favor. Thou art, in truth, the Lord of bounty, and the Sovereign of the kingdom of eternity.

- Baha'u'llah -

B

O Thou Whose face is the object of my adoration, Whose beauty is my sanctuary, Whose habitation is my goal, Whose praise is my hope, Whose providence is my companion, Whose love is the cause of my being, Whose mention is my solace, Whose nearness is my desire, Whose presence is my dearest wish and highest aspiration, I entreat Thee not to withhold from me the things Thou didst ordain for the chosen ones among Thy servants. Supply me, then, with the good of this world and of the next.

Thou, truly, art the King of all men. There is no God but Thee, the Ever-Forgiving, the Most Generous.

- Baha'u'llah -

C

Lord! Pitiful are we, grant us Thy favor; poor, bestow upon us a share from the ocean of Thy wealth; needy, do Thou satisfy us; abased, give us

Thy glory. The fowls of the air and the beasts of the field receive their meat each day from Thee, and all beings partake of Thy care and loving-kindness.

Deprive not this feeble one of Thy wondrous grace and vouchsafe by Thy might unto this helpless soul Thy bounty.

Give us our daily bread, and grant Thine increase in the necessities of life; that we may be dependent on none other but Thee, may commune wholly with Thee, may walk in Thy ways and declare Thy mysteries. Thou art the Almighty and the Loving and the Provider of all mankind.

- 'Abdu'l-Baha -

D

Remove not, O Lord, the festal board that hath been spread in Thy Name and extinguish not the burning flame that hath been kindled by Thine unquenchable fire. Withhold not from flowing that Living Water of Thine that murmureth with the melody of Thy glory and Thy remembrance, and deprive not Thy servants from the fragrance of Thy sweet savors breathing forth the perfume of Thy love.

Lord! Turn the distressing cares of Thy holy ones into ease, their hardship into comfort, their abasement into glory, their sorrow into blissful joy; O Thou that holdest in Thy grasp the reins of all mankind!

Thou art verily the One, the Single, the Mighty, the All-Knowing, the All-Wise.

- 'Abdu'l-Baha -

CHILDREN

A

O God, guide me, protect me, make of me a shining lamp and a brilliant star. Thou art the Mighty and the Powerful.

- 'Abdu'l-Baha -

B

O God my God! Bestow upon me a pure heart, like unto a pearl.

- 'Abdu'l-Baha -

C

O Thou pure God! I am a little child; make Thou the bosom of Thy Gift a dear resting-place of comfort, suffer me to grow and be nurtured with the honey and the milk of Thy love and train me under the breast of Thy knowledge; bestow Thou freedom while in a state of childhood and grant Thou excellence!

O Thou Incomparable One! Make me the confident of the Kingdom of the Unseen! Verily, Thou art the Mighty and the Powerful!

- 'Abdu'l-Baha -

D

Oh my Lord! O my Lord!

I am a child of tender years. Nourish me from the breast of Thy mercy, train me in the bosom of Thy love, educate me in the school of Thy guidance and develop me under the shadow of Thy bounty! Deliver me from darkness, make me a brilliant light; free me from unhappiness, make me a flower of the rose-garden; suffer me to become the servant of Thy Threshold and confer upon me the disposition and nature of the righteous ones; make me a cause of bounty to the human world and crown my head with the diadem of eternal life!

Verily, Thou art the Powerful, the Mighty, the Seer, the Hearer!

- 'Abdu'l-Baha -

E

O God! Educate these children. These children are the plants of Thine orchard, the flowers of Thy meadow, the roses of Thy garden. Let Thy rain fall upon them; let the Sun of Reality shine upon them with Thy love. Let Thy breeze refresh them in order that they may be trained, grow and develop and appear in the utmost beauty. Thou art the Giver! Thou art the Compassionate!

- 'Abdu'l-Baha -

F

O God! Rear this little babe in the bosom of Thy love and give it milk from the breast of Providence. Cultivate this fresh plant in the rose-garden of Thy love and nurture it by showers from the clouds of Providence. Make it a child of the Kingdom and lead it to the divine world. Thou art powerful and kind! Thou art the Giver, the Bestower, Whose blessings transcend all else!

- 'Abdu'l-Baha -

DAWN

A

O my God and my Master! I am Thy servant and the son of Thy servant. I have risen from my couch at this dawn-tide when the Day-star of Thy oneness hath shone forth from the Day-Spring of Thy will, and hath shed its radiance upon the whole world, according to what had been ordained in the Books of Thy Decree.

Praise be unto Thee, O my God, that we have wakened to the splendors of the light of Thy knowledge. Send down, then, upon us, O my Lord, what will enable us to dispense with any one but Thee, and will rid us of all attachment to aught except Thyself. Write down, moreover, for me, and for such as are dear to me, and for my kindred, man and woman alike, the good of this world and the world to come. Keep us safe, then, through Thine unfailing protection, O Thou the Beloved of the entire creation and the Desire of the whole universe, from them whom Thou hast made to be the manifestations of the evil whisperer, who whisper in men's breasts. Potent art Thou to do Thy pleasure. Thou art, verily, the Almighty, the Help in Peril, the Self-Subsisting.

Bless Thou, O Lord my God, Him Whom Thou hast set over Thy most excellent Titles, and through Whom Thou hast divided between the godly and the wicked, and graciously aid us to do what Thou lovest and desirest. Bless Thou, moreover, O my God, them Who are Thy Words and Thy Letters, and them who have set their faces towards Thee, and turned unto Thy face, and hearkened to Thy Call.

Thou art, verily, the Lord and King of all men, and art potent over all things.

- Baha'u'llah -

DAY OF GOD

A

Magnified be Thy Name, O my God, for that Thou hast manifested the Day which is the King of Days, the Day which Thou didst announce unto Thy chosen Ones and Thy Prophets in Thy most excellent Tablets, the Day whereon Thou didst shed the splendor of the glory of all Thy names upon all created things. Great is his blessedness whosoever hath set himself towards Thee, and entered Thy presence, and caught the accents of Thy voice.

I beseech Thee, O my Lord, by the name of Him round Whom circleth in adoration the kingdom of Thy names, that Thou wilt graciously assist them that are dear to Thee to glorify Thy word among Thy servants, and to shed abroad Thy praise amidst Thy creatures, so that the ecstasies of Thy Revelation may fill the souls of all the dwellers of Thine earth.

Since Thou hast guided them, O my Lord, unto the living waters of Thy grace, grant, by Thy bounty, that they may not be kept back from Thee; and since Thou hast summoned them to the habitation of Thy throne, drive them not out from Thy presence, through Thy loving-kindness. Send down upon them what shall wholly detach them from aught else except Thee, and make them able to soar in the atmosphere of Thy nearness, in such wise that neither the ascendancy of the oppressor nor the suggestions of them that have disbelieved in Thy most august and most mighty Self shall be capable of keeping them back from Thee.

- Baha'u'llah -

FOR THE DEPARTED

A

Glory be to Thee, O Lord my God! Abase not him whom Thou hast exalted through the power of Thine everlasting sovereignty, and remove not far from Thee him whom Thou hast caused to enter the tabernacle of Thine eternity. Wilt Thou cast away, O my God, him whom Thou hast overshadowed with Thy Lordship, and wilt Thou turn away from Thee, O my Desire, him to whom Thou hast been a refuge? Canst Thou degrade him whom Thou hast uplifted, or forget him whom Thou didst enable to remember Thee?

Glorified, immensely glorified art Thou! Thou art He Who from everlasting hath been the King of the entire creation and its Prime Mover, and Thou wilt to everlasting remain the Lord of all created things and their Ordainer. Glorified art Thou, O my God! If Thou ceasest to be merciful unto Thy servants, who, then, will show mercy unto them? and if Thou refusest to succor Thy loved ones, who is there that can succor them?

Glorified, immeasurably glorified art Thou! Thou art adored in Thy truth, and Thee do we all, verily, worship; and Thou art manifest in Thy justice, and to Thee do we all, verily, bear witness. Thou, art, in truth, beloved in Thy grace. No God is there but Thee, the Help in Peril, the Self-Subsisting.

- Baha'u'llah -

B

O my God! O Thou forgiver of sins! Bestower of gifts! Dispeller of afflictions!

Verily, I beseech Thee to forgive the sins of such as have abandoned the physical garment and have ascended to the spiritual world.

O my Lord! Purify them from trespasses, dispel their sorrows, and change their darkness into light.

Cause them to enter the garden of happiness, cleanse them with the most pure water, and grant them to behold Thy splendors on the loftiest mount.

- 'Abdu'l-Baha -

C

He is God, exalted is He, the Lord of loving-kindness and bounty!

Glory be unto Thee, Thou, O my God, the Lord Omnipotent. I testify to Thine omnipotence and Thy might, Thy sovereignty and Thy loving-kindness, Thy grace and Thy power, the oneness of Thy Being and the unity of Thine Essence, Thy sanctity and exaltation above the world of being and all that is therein.

O my God! Thou seest me detached from all save Thee, holding fast unto Thee and turning unto the ocean of Thy bounty, to the heaven of Thy favor, to the Daystar of Thy grace.

Lord! I bear witness that in Thy servant Thou hast reposed Thy Trust and that is the spirit wherewith Thou hast given life to the world.

I ask of Thee by the splendor of the Orb of Thy Revelation, mercifully to accept from him that which he hath achieved in Thy days. Grant then that he may be invested with the glory of Thy good-pleasure and adorned with Thine acceptance.

O my Lord! I myself and all created things bear witness unto Thy might and I pray Thee not to turn away from Thyself this spirit that hath ascended unto Thee, unto Thy heavenly place, Thine exalted Paradise and Thy retreats of nearness.

O Thou who art the Lord of all men! Grant then, O my God, that Thy servant may consort with Thy chosen ones, Thy saints and Thy Messengers in heavenly places that the pen cannot tell nor the tongue recount.

O My Lord, the poor one hath verily hastened unto the Kingdom of Thy wealth, the stranger unto his home within Thy precincts, he that is sore athirst to the heavenly river of Thy bounty. Deprive him not, O Lord, from his share of the banquet of Thy grace and from the favor of Thy bounty. Thou art in truth the Almighty, the Gracious, the All-Bountiful!

O my God, Thy trust hath been returned unto Thee. It behooveth Thy grace and Thy bounty that have compassed Thy dominions on earth and in heaven, to vouchsafe unto Thy newly welcomed one Thy gifts and Thy bestowals, and the fruits of the tree of Thy grace! Powerful art Thou to do as Thou willest. There is none other God but Thee, the Gracious, the Most Bountiful, the Compassionate, the Bestower, the Pardoner, the Precious, the All-Knowing.

I testify, O my Lord, that Thou hast enjoined upon men to honor their guest, and he that hath ascended unto Thee hath verily reached Thee and attained Thy Presence. Deal with him then according to Thy grace and bounty! By Thy glory, I know of a certainty that Thou wilt not deny Thyself from that which Thou hast commanded Thy servants, nor wilt Thou deprive him that hath clung to the cord of Thy bounty and hath ascended to the Day-Spring of Thy wealth.

There is none other God but Thee, the One, the Single, the Powerful, the Omniscient, the Bountiful.

- Baha'u'llah -

DREAMS

A

O thou bird of the Garden of God!

Why art thou sad and sorrowful, disappointed and grieved! Praise be to God! the eternal bounty is in succession, the Divine Glory is apparent and manifest, the display of Providence and Light of Guidance is glistening and shining from the Kingdom of ABHA and the appearance of the Greatest Sun is clear and evident. If thou art outwardly far, then thou art near in spirit, and if thou art absent in body, thou art present in heart and spirit.

Arise and wash thy body, wear a pure gown, and, directing thyself to the Kingdom of God, supplicate and pray to Him. Sleep in a clean, well prepared and ventilated place, and ask for appearance (or display) in the World of Vision. Thou wilt have visions which will cause the doors of doubts to be closed, which will give thee new joy, wonderful dilation, brilliant glory. Thou wilt comprehend realities and meanings.

Verily, the bounty of the Kingdom is unlimited and the favors of the Lord of Majesty are like unto the rains of springtime.

- 'Abdu'l-Baha -

B

O thou who art cheered through the Fragrances of God!

When thou desirest and yearnest for meeting in the World of Vision; at the time when thou art in perfect fragrance and spirituality, wash thy hands and face, clothe thyself in clean robes, turn toward the court of the Peerless One, offer prayer to Him and lay thy head upon the pillow. When sleep cometh, the doors of revelation shall be opened and all thy desires shall become revealed!

Endeavor to guide thy mother and confirm her in faith; when the heart becometh confident, the imagination of Satan and evil vanisheth away. If the heart becometh absolutely tranquil, suspicion and imagination will entirely pass away.

- 'Abdu'l-Baha -

C

If anyone should have a troubled dream and thereby be saddened and grieved reciting this blessed verse has been decreed:

O God, by Thy Name through which the Sea of Ecstasy moveth and the Fragrances of Thy manifold delights are wafted! I beseech Thee by the wonders of Thy grace to reveal unto me that which shall brighten my eyes and gladden my heart. Verily, Thou art the Giver, the Generous.

Reciting this verse is effective even in the case of dreams which are not troubled.

- Baha'u'llah -

EVENING

A

O my God, my Master, the Goal of my desire! This, Thy servant, seeketh to sleep in the shelter of Thy mercy, and to repose beneath the canopy of Thy grace, imploring Thy care and Thy protection.

I beg of Thee, O my Lord, by Thine eye that sleepeth not, to guard mine eyes from beholding aught beside Thee. Strengthen, then, their vision that they may discern Thy signs, and behold the Horizon of Thy Revelation. Thou art He before the revelations of Whose omnipotence the quintessence of power hath trembled.

No God is there but Thee, the Almighty, the All-Subduing, the Unconditioned.

- Baha'u'llah -

B

How can I choose to sleep, O God, my God, when the eyes of them that long for Thee are wakeful because of their separation from Thee; and how can I lie down to rest whilst the souls of Thy lovers are sore vexed in their remoteness from Thy presence?

I have committed, O my Lord, my spirit and my entire being into the right hand of Thy might and Thy protection, and I lay my head on my pillow through Thy power, and lift it up according to Thy will and Thy good-pleasure. Thou art, in truth, the Preserver, the Keeper, the Almighty, the Most Powerful.

By Thy might! I ask not, whether sleeping or waking, but that which Thou dost desire. I am Thy servant and in Thy hands. Do Thou graciously aid me to do what will shed forth the fragrance of Thy good pleasure. This, truly, is my hope and the hope of them that enjoy near access to Thee. Praised be Thou, O Lord of the worlds!

- Baha'u'llah -

C

O seeker of Truth! If thou desirest that God may open thine eye, thou must supplicate unto God, pray to and commune with Him at midnight, saying:

O Lord, I have turned my face unto Thy Kingdom of oneness and am immersed in the sea of Thy mercy! O Lord, enlighten my sight by beholding Thy lights in this dark night, and make me happy by the wine of Thy love in this wonderful age! O Lord, make me hear Thy call, and open before my face the doors of Thy heaven, so that I may see the light of Thy glory and become attracted to Thy beauty!

Verily, Thou art the Giver, the Generous, the Merciful, the Forgiving!

- 'Abdu'l-Baha -

FORGIVENESS

A

Glorified art Thou, O Lord my God! I beseech Thee by Thy chosen Ones, and by the Bearers of Thy Trust, and by Him Whom Thou hast ordained to be the Seal of Thy Prophets and of Thy Messengers, to let Thy remembrance be my companion, and Thy love my aim, and Thy face my goal, and Thy Name my lamp, and Thy wish my desire, and Thy pleasure my delight.

I am a sinner, O my Lord, and Thou art the Ever-Forgiving. As soon as I recognized Thee, I hastened to attain the exalted court of Thy loving-kindness. Forgive me, O my Lord, my sins which have hindered me from walking in the ways of Thy good-pleasure, and from attaining the shores of the ocean of Thy oneness.

There is no one, O my Lord, who can deal bounti-fully with me to whom I can turn my face, and none who can have compassion on me that I may crave his mercy. Cast me not out, I implore Thee, of the presence of Thy grace, neither do Thou withhold from me the outpourings of Thy generosity and bounty. Ordain for me, O my Lord, what Thou hast ordained for them that love Thee, and write down for me what Thou hast written down for Thy chosen ones. My gaze hath, at all times, been fixed on the horizon of Thy gracious providence, and mine eyes bent upon the court of Thy tender mercies. Do with me as beseemeth Thee. No God is there but Thee, the God of power, the God of glory, Whose help is implored by all men.

- Baha'u'llah -

B

I am He, O my Lord, that hath set his face towards Thee, and fixed his hope on the wonders of Thy grace and the revelations of Thy bounty. I pray Thee that Thou wilt not suffer me to turn away disappointed from the door of Thy mercy, nor abandon me to such of Thy creatures as have repudiated Thy Cause.

I am, O my God, Thy servant and the son of Thy servant. I have recognized Thy truth in Thy days, and have directed my steps toward the shores of Thy oneness, confessing Thy singleness, acknowledging Thy unity, and hoping for Thy forgiveness and pardon. Powerful art Thou to do what Thou willest; no God is there beside Thee, the All-Glorious, the Ever-Forgiving.

- Baha'u'llah -

C

Thou seest me, O my Lord, with my face turned toward the heaven of Thy bounty and the ocean of Thy favor, withdrawn from all else beside Thee. I ask of Thee, by the splendors of the Sun of Thy Revelation on Sinai, and the effulgences of the Orb of Thy grace which shineth from the horizon of Thy Name, the Ever-Forgiving, to grant me Thy pardon and to have mercy upon me. Write down, then, for me with Thy pen of glory that which will exalt me through Thy Name in the world of creation. Aid me, O my Lord, to set myself toward Thee, and to hearken unto the voice of Thy loved ones, whom the powers of the earth have failed to weaken, and the dominion of the nations has been powerless to withhold from Thee, and who, advancing toward Thee, have said: "God is our Lord, the Lord of all who are in heaven and all who are on earth!"

- Baha'u'llah -

D

Lauded be Thy Name, O my God and the God of all things, my Glory and the Glory of all things, my Desire and the Desire of all things, my Strength and the Strength of all things, my King and the King of all things, my Possessor and the Possessor of all things, my Aim and the Aim of all things, my Mover and the Mover of all things! Suffer me not, I implore Thee, to be kept back from the ocean of Thy tender mercies, nor to be far removed from the shores of nearness to Thee.

Aught else except Thee, O my Lord, profiteth me not, and near access to any one save Thyself availeth me nothing. I entreat Thee by the plenteousness of Thy riches, whereby Thou didst dispense with all else except Thyself, to number me with such as have set their faces towards Thee, and arisen to serve Thee.

Forgive, then, O my Lord, Thy servants and Thy handmaidens. Thou, truly, art the Ever-Forgiving, the Most Compassionate.

- Baha'u'llah -

E

O Lord! O Thou hope of people! Thou art the shelter of all these Thy servants. Thou knowest the secrets and mysteries. We are all sinners and Thou art the shelter of sinners, the Merciful, the Clement. O Lord! look not at our shortcomings. Deal with us according to Thy grace and bestowal. Our shortcomings are many but the ocean of Thy forgiveness is boundless. Therefore confirm and strengthen us. Assist us in that which will make us acceptable at Thy threshold. Illumine the hearts, make the eyes seeing, render the ears attentive, resuscitate the dead and heal the sick. Render the poor rich and the fugitive confident. Accept us in Thy Kingdom. Illumine us with the light of kindness. Thou art the Generous! Thou art the Clement! Thou art the Kind!

- 'Abdu'l-Baha -

HEALING

A

O God, my God! I beg of Thee by the ocean of Thy healing, and by the splendors of the Day-Star of Thy grace, and by Thy Name through which Thou didst subdue Thy servants, and by the pervasive power of Thy most exalted Word and the potency of Thy most august Pen, and by Thy mercy that hath preceded the creation of all who are in heaven and on earth, to purge me with the waters of Thy bounty from every affliction and disorder, and from all weakness and feebleness.

Thou seest, O my Lord, Thy suppliant waiting at the door of Thy bounty, and him who hath set his hopes on Thee clinging to the cord of Thy generosity. Deny him not, I beseech Thee, the things he seeketh from the ocean of Thy grace and the Day-Star of Thy loving-kindness.

Powerful art Thou to do what pleaseth Thee. There is none other God save Thee, the Ever-Forgiving, the Most Generous.

- Baha'u'llah -

B

Thy Name is my healing, O my God, and remembrance of Thee is my remedy. Nearness to Thee is my hope, and love for Thee is my companion. Thy mercy to me is my healing and my succor in both this world and the world to come. Thou, verily, art the All-Bountiful, the All-Knowing, the All-Wise.

- Baha'u'llah -

C

Praised be Thou, O Lord my God! I implore Thee by Thy Most Great Name through Which Thou didst stir up Thy servants and build up Thy cities, and by Thy most excellent titles, and Thy most august attributes, to assist Thy people to turn in the direction of Thy manifold bounties, and set their faces toward the Tabernacle of Thy wisdom. Heal Thou the sicknesses that have assailed the souls on every side, and have deterred them from directing their gaze toward the Paradise that lieth in the shelter of Thy shadowing Name, which Thou didst ordain to be the King of all names unto all who are in heaven and all who are on earth. Potent art Thou to do as pleaseth Thee. In Thy hands is the empire of all names. There is none other God but Thee, the Mighty, the Wise.

I am but a poor creature, O my Lord; I have clung to the hem of Thy riches. I am sore sick; I have held fast the cord of Thy healing. Deliver me from the ills that have encircled me, and wash me thoroughly with the waters of Thy graciousness and mercy, and attire me with the raiment of wholesomeness, through Thy forgiveness and bounty. Fix, then, mine eyes upon Thee, and rid me of all attachment to aught else except Thyself. Aid me to do what Thou desirest, and to fulfill what Thou pleasest.

Thou art truly the Lord of this life and of the next. Thou art, in truth, the Ever-Forgiving, the Most Merciful.

- Baha'u'llah -

D

Glory be to Thee, O Lord my God! I implore Thee by Thy Name, through which Thou didst lift up the ensigns of Thy guidance, and didst shed the radiance of Thy loving-kindness, and didst reveal the sovereignty of Thy Lordship; through which the lamp of Thy names hath appeared within the niche of Thine attributes, and He Who is the Tabernacle of Thy unity and the Manifestation of detachment hath shone forth; through which the ways of Thy guidance were made known, and the paths of Thy good pleasure were marked out; through which the foundations of error have been made to tremble, and the signs of wickedness have been abolished; through which the fountains of wisdom have burst forth, and the heavenly table hath been sent down; through which Thou didst preserve Thy servants and didst vouchsafe Thy healing; through which Thou didst show forth Thy tender mercies unto Thy servants and revealedst Thy forgiveness amidst Thy creatures—I implore Thee to keep safe him who hath held fast and returned unto Thee, and clung to Thy mercy, and seized the hem of Thy loving providence. Send down, then, upon him Thy healing, and make him whole, and endue him with a constancy vouchsafed by Thee, and a tranquillity bestowed by Thy Highness.

Thou art, verily, the Healer, the Preserver, the Helper, the Almighty, the Powerful, the All-Glorious, the All-Knowing.

- *Baha'u'llah* -

E

Glory be to Thee, O Lord my God! I beg of Thee by Thy Name through which He Who is Thy Beauty hath been stablished upon the throne of Thy Cause, and by Thy Name through which Thou changest all things, and gatherest together all things, and callest to account all things, and rewardest all things, and preservest all things, and sustainest all things--I beg of Thee to guard this handmaiden who hath fled for refuge to Thee, and hath sought the shelter of Him in Whom Thou Thyself art manifest, and hath put her whole trust and confidence in Thee.

She is sick, O my God, and hath entered beneath the shadow of the Tree of Thy healing; afflicted, and hath fled to the City of Thy protection;

diseased, and hath sought the Fountain-Head of Thy favors; sorely vexed, and hath hasted to attain the Well-Spring of Thy tranquillity; burdened with sin, and hath set her face toward the court of Thy forgiveness.

Attire her, by Thy sovereignty and Thy loving-kindness, O my God and my Beloved, with the raiment of Thy balm and Thy healing, and make her quaff of the cup of Thy mercy and Thy favors. Protect her, moreover, from every affliction and ailment, from all pain and sickness, and from whatsoever may be abhorrent unto Thee.

Thou, in truth, art immensely exalted above all else except Thyself. Thou art, verily, the Healer, the All-Sufficing, the Preserver, the Ever-Forgiving, the Most Merciful.

- Baha'u'llah -

MANKIND

A

My God, Whom I worship and adore! I bear witness unto Thy unity and Thy oneness, and acknowledge Thy gifts, both in the past and in the present. Thou art the All-Bountiful, the overflowing showers of Whose mercy have rained down upon high and low alike, and the splendors of Whose grace have been shed over both the obedient and the rebellious.

O God of mercy, before Whose door the quintessence of mercy hath bowed down, and round the sanctuary of Whose Cause loving-kindness, in its inmost spirit, hath circled, we beseech Thee, entreating Thine ancient grace, and seeking Thy present favor, that Thou mayest have mercy upon all who are the manifestation of the world of being, and to deny them not the outpourings of Thy grace in Thy days.

All are but poor and needy, and Thou, verily, art the All-Possessing, the All-Subduing, the All-Powerful.

- Baha'u'llah -

B

Lauded be Thy Name, O Lord my God! Darkness hath fallen upon every land, and the forces of mischief have encompassed all the nations. Through them, however, I perceive the splendors of Thy wisdom, and discern the brightness of the light of Thy providence.

They that are shut out as by a veil from Thee have imagined that they have the power to put out Thy light, and to quench Thy fire, and to still the winds of Thy grace. Nay, and to this Thy might beareth me witness! Had not every tribulation been made the bearer of Thy wisdom, and every ordeal the vehicle of Thy providence, no one would have dared oppose us, though the powers of earth and heaven were to be leagued against us. Were I to unravel the wondrous mysteries of Thy wisdom which are laid bare before me, the reins of Thine enemies would be cleft asunder.

Glorified be Thou, then, O my God! I beseech Thee by Thy Most Great Name to assemble them that love Thee around the Law that streameth from the good-pleasure of Thy will, and to send down upon them what will assure their hearts.

Potent art Thou to do what pleaseth Thee. Thou art, verily, the Help in Peril, the Self-Subsisting.

- Baha'u'llah -

C

O kind Lord! Thou Who art generous and merciful! We are the servants of Thy threshold and we are under the protection of Thy mercy. The Sun of Thy providence is shining upon all and the clouds of Thy mercy shower upon all. Thy gifts encompass all, Thy providence sustains all, Thy protection overshadows all and the glances of Thy favor illumine all. O Lord! Grant unto us Thine infinite bestowals and let Thy light of guidance shine. Illumine the eyes, make joyous the souls and confer a new spirit upon the hearts. Give them eternal life. Open the doors of Thy knowledge; let the light of faith shine. Unite and bring mankind into one shelter beneath the banner of Thy protection, so that they may become as waves of one sea, as leaves and branches of one tree, and may assemble beneath the shadow of the same tent. May they drink from the same fountain. May they be refreshed by the same breezes. May they obtain illumination from the same source of light and life. Thou art the Giver, the Merciful!

- 'Abdu'l-Baha -

D

O Thou compassionate Lord! Thou Who art generous and able! We are servants of Thine sheltered beneath Thy providence. Cast Thy glance of favor upon us. Give light to our eyes, hearing to our ears and understanding and love to our hearts. Render our souls joyous and happy through Thy glad-tidings. O Lord! Point out to us the pathway of Thy Kingdom and resuscitate all of us through the breaths of the Holy Spirit. Bestow upon us life everlasting and confer upon us never-ending honor. Unify mankind and illumine the world of humanity. May we all follow Thy pathway, long for Thy good-pleasure and seek the mysteries of Thy Kingdom. O God! Unite us and connect our hearts with Thy indissoluble bond. Verily, Thou art the Giver, Thou art the Kind One and Thou art the Almighty.

- 'Abdu'l-Baha -

E

O Thou kind Lord! Thou hast created all humanity from the same original parents. Thou hast intended that all belong to the same household. In Thy Holy Presence they are Thy servants and all mankind are sheltered beneath Thy Tabernacle. All have gathered at Thy table of bounty and are radiant through the light of Thy providence. O God! Thou art kind to all, Thou hast provided for all, Thou dost shelter all, Thou dost confer life upon all. Thou hast endowed all with talents and faculties; all are submerged in the ocean of Thy mercy. O Thou kind Lord! unite all, let the religions agree, make the nations one so that they may be as one kind and as children of the same fatherland. May they associate in unity and concord. O God! upraise the standard of the oneness of humankind. O God! establish the Most Great Peace.

Cement the hearts together, O God! O Thou kind Father, God! exhilarate the hearts through the fragrance of Thy love; brighten the eyes through the light of Thy guidance; cheer the hearing with the melodies of Thy Word and shelter us in the cave of Thy providence. Thou art the Mighty and Powerful! Thou art the Forgiving and Thou art the One Who overlooketh the shortcomings of humankind.

- 'Abdu'l-Baha -

MEALS

A

O Lord! Confirm and aid this assemblage. Confirm these souls through the breaths of Thy Holy Spirit. Enlighten the eyes by the vision of these radiant lights, and make the ears joyful through the anthems of Thy call to service. O God! Verily, we have gathered here in the fragrance of Thy love. We have turned to Thy Kingdom. We seek naught save Thee and desire nothing save Thy good pleasure. O God! Let this food be Thy manna from heaven, and grant that this assemblage may be a concourse of Thy supreme ones. May they be the quickening cause of love to humanity and the source of illumination to the human race. May they be the instruments of Thy guidance upon earth. Verily,

Thou art powerful. Thou art the Bestower. Thou art the Forgiver, and Thou art the Almighty.

- 'Abdu'l-Baha -

B

At lunch:

He is God! Thou seest us, O my God, gathered around this table, praising Thy bounty, with our gaze set upon Thy Kingdom. O Lord! Send down upon us Thy heavenly food and confer upon us Thy blessing. Thou art verily the Bestower, the Merciful, the Compassionate.

- 'Abdu'l-Baha -

C

At the dinner table:

He is God! How can we render Thee thanks, O Lord? Thy bounties are endless and our gratitude cannot equal them. How can the finite utter praise of the Infinite? Unable are we to voice our thanks for Thy favors and in utter powerlessness we turn wholly to Thy Kingdom beseeching the increase of Thy bestowals and bounties. Thou art the Giver, the Bestower, the Almighty.

- 'Abdu'l-Baha -

D

To be recited before eating:

O my Lord and my Hope! Praise be to Thee that Thou hast sent down upon us this spiritual table, this heavenly blessing, this divine bounty. O our Lord, enable us to eat of this food of Thy Kingdom that its subtle essences may permeate the recesses of our spiritual being producing heavenly strength for service in Thy Cause, the spreading of Thy revelation, and the adorning of Thy garden with lofty trees, perfumed with fresh breezes and fruit-bearing branches near at hand. Verily, Thou art the All-Generous, the Possessor of Infinite Grace. Thou art the Merciful, the Compassionate.

- 'Abdu'l-Baha -

E

To be recited after eating:

O my Lord and my Hope! Thanks be to Thee for these bestowals and these bounties. Lord, Lord, raise us up unto Thy Kingdom and seat us at the tables of Thy realm on high. Give us to eat of the food of Thy presence and give us to taste of the sweetness of beholding Thy beauty! This, in truth, is our highest wish and Thy greatest bestowal and most mighty bounty. Lord, Lord, make this easy for us. Verily, Thou art the Generous, the Bountiful! Thou art the Giver, the Mighty, the Compassionate.

- 'Abdu'l-Baha -

MEETINGS

A

Glorified art Thou, O Lord my God! I implore Thee by the onrushing winds of Thy grace, and by them Who are the Day-Springs of Thy purpose and the Dawning-Places of Thine inspiration, to send down upon me and upon all that have sought Thy face that which beseemeth Thy generosity and bountiful grace, and is worthy of Thy bestowals and favor. Poor and desolate I am, O my Lord! Immerse me in the ocean of Thy wealth; athirst, suffer me to drink from the living water of Thy loving-kindness.

I beseech Thee, by Thine own Self and by Him Whom Thou hast appointed as the Manifestation of Thine own Being and Thy discriminating Word unto all that are in heaven and on earth, to gather together Thy servants beneath the shade of the Tree of Thy gracious providence. Help them, then, to partake of its fruits, to incline their ears to the rustling of its leaves, and to the sweetness of the voice of the Bird that chanteth upon its branches. Thou art, verily, the Help in Peril, the Inaccessible, the Almighty, the Most Bountiful.

- Bahá'u'lláh -

B

O Thou merciful God! O Thou Who art mighty and powerful! O Thou most kind Father! These servants have gathered together, turning to Thee, supplicating Thy threshold, desiring Thine endless bounties from Thy great assurance. They have no purpose save Thy good-pleasure. They have no intention save service to the world of humanity. O God! Make this assemblage radiant. Make the hearts merciful. Confer the bounties of the Holy Spirit. Endow them with a power from heaven. Bless them with heavenly minds. Increase their sincerity so that with all humility and contrition they may turn to Thy Kingdom and be occupied with service to the world of humanity. May each one become a radiant candle. May each one become a brilliant star. May each one become beautiful in color and redolent of fragrance in the Kingdom of God. O kind Father! Confer Thy blessings. Consider not our shortcomings. Shelter us under Thy protection. Remember not our sins. Heal us with Thy mercy. We are weak; Thou art mighty. We are poor; Thou art rich. We are sick; Thou art the Physician. We are needy; Thou art most generous. O God! Endow us with Thy providence. Thou art the Powerful! Thou art the Giver! Thou art the Beneficent!

- *'Abdu'l-Baha* -

C

O Thou kind Lord! These are Thy servants who have gathered in this meeting, turned unto Thy Kingdom and are in need of Thy bestowal and blessing. O Thou God! Manifest and make evident the signs of Thy oneness which have been deposited in all the realities of life. Reveal and unfold the virtues which Thou hast made latent and concealed in these human realities. O God! We are as plants and Thy bounty is as the rain. Refresh and cause these plants to grow through Thy bestowal. We are

Thy servants; free us from the fetters of material existence. We are ignorant; make us wise. We are dead; make us alive. We are material; endow us with spirit. We are deprived; make us the intimates of Thy mysteries. We are needy; enrich and bless us from Thy boundless treasury. O God! Resuscitate us, give us sight, give us hearing. Familiarize us with the mysteries of life, so that the secrets of Thy kingdom may become revealed to us in this world of existence and we may confess Thy oneness. Every bestowal emanates from Thee; every benediction is Thine. Thou art mighty! Thou art powerful! Thou art the Giver and Thou art the Ever-Bounteous!

- 'Abdu'l-Baha -

D

O my God! O my God! Verily these servants are turning to Thee, supplicating Thy kingdom of mercy. Verily, they are attracted by Thy holiness and set aglow with the fire of Thy love, seeking confirmation from Thy wondrous Kingdom, and hoping for attainment in Thy heavenly realm. Verily they long for the descent of Thy bestowal, desiring illumination from the Sun of Reality. O Lord! make them radiant lamps, merciful signs, fruitful trees and shining stars. May they come forth in Thy service and be connected with Thee by the bonds and ties of Thy love, longing for the lights of Thy favor. O Lord! make them signs of guidance, standards of Thy immortal Kingdom, waves of the sea of Thy mercy, mirrors of the light of Thy majesty.

Verily Thou art the Generous. Verily Thou art the Merciful. Verily Thou art the Precious, the Beloved!

- 'Abdu'l-Baha -

E

O Thou forgiving God! These servants are turning to Thy kingdom and seeking Thy grace and bounty. O God! Make their hearts good and pure in order that they may become worthy of Thy love. Purify and sanctify the spirits that the light of the Sun of Reality may shine through them. Purify and sanctify the eyes that they may perceive Thy lights. Purify and sanctify the ears in order that they may hear the call of Thy Kingdom. O Lord! Verily we are weak but Thou art mighty. Verily we are poor but Thou art rich. We are seekers and Thou art the one sought. O Lord! have compassion upon us and forgive us; bestow upon us capacity and readiness in order that we may be responsive to Thy favors, attracted to Thy Kingdom, enkindled with the fire of Thy love and resuscitated through the breaths of Thy Holy Spirit in this radiant century. Thou art powerful; Thou art almighty; Thou art merciful; and Thou art most generous!

- 'Abdu'l-Baha -

MORNING

A

I have wakened in Thy shelter, O my God, and it becometh him that seeketh that shelter to abide within the Sanctuary of Thy protection and the Stronghold of Thy defense. Illumine my inner being, O my Lord, with the splendors of the Day-Spring of Thy Revelation, even as Thou didst illumine my outer being with the morning light of Thy favor.

- Baha'u'llah -

B

I have risen this morning by Thy grace, O my God, and left my home trusting wholly in Thee, and committing myself to Thy care. Send down, then, upon me, out of the heaven of Thy mercy, a blessing from Thy side, and enable me to return home in safety even as Thou didst enable me to set out under Thy protection with my thoughts fixed steadfastly upon Thee.

There is none other God but Thee, the One, the Incomparable, the All-Knowing, the All-Wise.

- Baha'u'llah -

C

I give praise to Thee, O my God, that Thou hast awakened me out of my sleep, and brought me forth after my disappearance, and raised me up from my slumber. I have wakened this morning with my face set toward the splendors of the Day-Star of Thy Revelation, through which the heavens of Thy power and Thy majesty have been illumined, acknowledging Thy signs, believing in Thy Book, and holding fast unto Thy Cord.

I beseech Thee, by the potency of Thy will and the compelling power of Thy purpose, to make of what Thou didst reveal unto me in my sleep the surest foundation for the mansions of Thy love that are within the hearts of Thy loved ones, and the best instrument for the revelation of the tokens of Thy grace and Thy loving-kindness.

Do Thou ordain for me through Thy most exalted Pen, O my Lord, the good of this world and of the next. I testify that within Thy grasp are held the reins of all things. Thou changest them as Thou pleasest. No God is there save Thee, the Strong, the Faithful.

Thou art He Who changeth through His bidding abasement into glory, and weakness into strength, and powerlessness into might, and fear into calm, and doubt into certainty. No God is there but Thee, the Mighty, the Beneficent.

Thou disappointest no one who hath sought Thee, nor dost Thou keep back from Thee any one who hath desired Thee. Ordain Thou for me what becometh the heaven of Thy generosity, and the ocean of Thy bounty. Thou art, verily, the Almighty, the Most Powerful.

- Baha'u'llah -

NOONDAY

A

To be recited once in twenty four hours, at noon.

Whoso wisheth to recite this prayer, let him stand up and turn [facing the qiblih] unto God, and, then let him say:

O God, I bear witness that Thou hast created me to know Thee and to adore Thee. I testify, at this moment, to my poverty and to Thy Wealth, to my weakness and to Thy Strength. Indeed there is no other God but Thee, the Help in Peril, the Self-Subsisting.

- Baha'u'llah -

By 'morning', 'noon', and 'evening,' mentioned in connection with the Obligatory Prayers, is meant respectively the intervals between sunrise and noon, between noon and sunset, and from sunset until two hours after sunset.

PARENTS

A

Thou seest, O Lord, our suppliant hands lifted up towards the heaven of Thy favor and bounty. Grant that they may be filled with the treasures of Thy munificence and bountiful favor. Forgive us, and our fathers, and our mothers, and fulfill whatsoever we have desired from the ocean of Thy grace and Divine generosity. Accept, O Beloved of our hearts, all our works in Thy path. Thou art, verily, the Most Powerful, the Most Exalted, the Incomparable, the One, the Forgiving, the Gracious.

- Baha'u'llah -

B

O Thou Almighty! O Thou Forgiver! O Thou Omnipotent Lord! In this Great

Dispensation Thou dost accept the intercession of the sons in behalf of their fathers. This is one of the special infinite bestowals of this cycle. Therefore, O Thou kind Almighty! Accept the request of this thy servant at the Threshold of Thy Singleness and submerge his father in the ocean of Thy graces--because this son is confirmed in the accomplishment of Thy services and is displaying the utmost of effort at all times in the pathway of Thy love! Verily Thou art the Giver, the Forgiver and the Kind!

- 'Abdu'l-Baha -

PRAISE AND GRATITUDE

A

Magnified be Thy Name, O Lord my God! Thou art He Whom all things worship and Who worshipeth no one, Who is the Lord of all things and is the vassal of none, Who knoweth all things and is known of none. Thou didst wish to make Thyself known unto men; therefore, Thou didst, through a word of Thy mouth, bring creation into being and fashion the universe. There is none other God except Thee, the Fashioner, the Creator, the Almighty, the Most Powerful.

I implore Thee, by this very word that hath shone forth above the horizon of Thy will, to enable me to drink deep of the living waters through which Thou hast vivified the hearts of Thy chosen ones and quickened the souls of them that love Thee, that I may, at all times and under all conditions, turn my face wholly towards Thee.

Thou art the God of power, of glory and bounty. No God is there beside Thee, the Supreme Ruler, the All-Glorious, the Omniscient.

- Baha'u'llah -

B

All praise, O my God, be to Thee Who art the Source of all glory and majesty, of greatness and honor, of sovereignty and dominion, of loftiness and grace, of awe and power. Whomsoever Thou willest Thou causest to draw nigh unto the Most Great Ocean, and on whomsoever Thou desirest Thou conferrest the honor of recognizing Thy Most Ancient Name. Of all who are in heaven and on earth, none can withstand the operation of Thy sovereign Will. From all eternity Thou didst rule the entire creation, and Thou wilt continue for evermore to exercise Thy dominion over all created things. There is none other God but Thee, the Almighty, the Most Exalted, the All-Powerful, the All-Wise.

Illumine, O Lord, the faces of Thy servants, that they may behold Thee; and cleanse their hearts that they may turn unto the court of Thy heavenly favors, and recognize Him Who is the Manifestation of Thy Self and the Day-Spring of Thine Essence. Verily, Thou art the Lord of all worlds. There is no God but Thee, the Unconstrained, the All-Subduing.

- *Baha'u'llah* -

C

Glorified art Thou, O Lord my God! I yield Thee thanks for having enabled me to recognize the Manifestation of Thyself, and for having severed me from Thine enemies, and laid bare before mine eyes their misdeeds and wicked works in Thy days, and for having rid me of all attachment to them, and caused me to turn wholly towards Thy grace and bountiful favors. I give Thee thanks, also, for having sent down upon me from the clouds of Thy will that which hath so sanctified me from the hints of the infidels and the allusions of the misbelievers that I have fixed my heart firmly on Thee, and fled from such as have denied the light of Thy countenance. Again I thank Thee for having empowered me to be steadfast in Thy love, and to speak forth Thy praise and to extol Thy virtues, and for having given me to drink of the cup of Thy mercy that hath surpassed all things visible and invisible.

Thou art the Almighty, the Most Exalted, the All-Glorious, the All-Loving.

- Baha'u'llah -

D

In the Name of God, the Most High! Lauded and glorified art Thou, Lord, God Omnipotent! Thou before Whose wisdom the wise falleth short and faileth, before Whose knowledge the learned confesseth his ignorance, before Whose might the strong waxeth weak, before Whose wealth the rich testifieth to his poverty, before Whose light the enlightened is lost in darkness, toward the shrine of Whose knowledge turneth the essence of all understanding and around the sanctuary of Whose presence circle the souls of all mankind.

How then can I sing and tell of Thine Essence, which the wisdom of the wise and the learning of the learned have failed to comprehend, inasmuch as no man can sing that which he understandeth not, nor recount that unto which he cannot attain, whilst thou hast been from everlasting the Inaccessible, the Unsearchable. Powerless though I be to rise to the heavens of Thy glory and soar in the realms of Thy knowledge, I can but recount Thy tokens that tell of Thy glorious handiwork.

By Thy Glory! O Beloved of all hearts, Thou that alone canst still the pangs of yearning for Thee! Though all the dwellers of heaven and earth unite to glorify the least of Thy signs, wherein and whereby Thou hast revealed Thyself, yet would they fail, how much more to praise Thy holy Word, the creator of all Thy tokens.

All praise and glory be to Thee, Thou of Whom all things have testified that Thou art one and there is none other God but Thee, Who hast been from everlasting exalted above all peer or likeness and to everlasting shalt remain the same. All kings are but Thy servants and all beings, visible and invisible, as naught before Thee. There is none other God but Thee, the Gracious, the Powerful, the Most High.

- *'Abdu'l-Baha* -

PRAYER FOR AMERICA

A

O Thou kind Lord! This gathering is turning to Thee. These hearts are radiant with Thy love. These minds and spirits are exhilarated by the message of Thy glad-tidings. O God! Let this American democracy become glorious in spiritual degrees even as it has aspired to material degrees, and render this just government victorious. Confirm this revered nation to upraise the standard of the oneness of humanity, to promulgate the Most Great Peace, to become thereby most glorious and praiseworthy among all the nations of the world. O God! This American nation is worthy of Thy favors and is deserving of Thy mercy. Make it precious and near to Thee through Thy bounty and bestowal.

- 'Abdu'l-Baha -

PROTECTION

A

Praised be Thou, O Lord my God! This is Thy servant who hath quaffed from the hands of Thy grace the wine of Thy tender mercy, and tasted of the savor of Thy love in Thy days. I beseech Thee, by the embodiments of Thy names whom no grief can hinder from rejoicing in Thy love or from gazing on Thy face, and whom all the hosts of the heedless are powerless to cause to turn aside from the path of Thy pleasure, to supply him with the good things Thou dost possess, and to raise him up to such heights that he will regard the world even as a shadow that vanisheth swifter than the twinkling of an eye.

Keep him safe also, O my God, by the power of Thine immeasurable majesty, from all that Thou abhorrest. Thou art, verily, his Lord and the Lord of all worlds.

- Baha'u'llah -

B

O God, my God! I have set out from my home, holding fast unto the cord of Thy love, and I have committed myself wholly to Thy care and Thy protection. I entreat Thee by Thy power through which Thou didst protect Thy loved ones from the wayward and the perverse, and from every contumacious oppressor, and every wicked doer who hath strayed far from Thee, to keep me safe by Thy bounty and Thy grace. Enable me, then, to return to my home by Thy power and Thy might. Thou art, truly, the Almighty, the Help in Peril, the Self-Subsisting.

- Baha'u'llah -

C

Praise be to Thee, O Lord my God! Thou seest and knowest that I have called upon Thy servants to turn nowhere except in the direction of Thy bestowals, and have bidden them observe naught save the things Thou didst prescribe in Thy

Perspicuous Book, the Book which hath been sent down according to Thine inscrutable decree and irrevocable purpose.

I can utter no word, O my God, unless I be permitted by Thee, and can move in no direction until I obtain Thy sanction. It is Thou, O my God, Who hast called me into being through the power of Thy might, and hast endued me with Thy grace to manifest Thy Cause. Wherefore I have been subjected to such adversities that my tongue hath been hindered from extolling Thee and from magnifying Thy glory.

All praise be to Thee, O my God, for the things Thou didst ordain for me through Thy decree and by the power of Thy sovereignty. I beseech Thee that thou wilt fortify both myself and them that love me in our love for Thee, and wilt keep us firm in Thy Cause. I swear by Thy might! O my God! Thy servant's shame is to be shut out as by a veil from Thee, and his glory is to know Thee. Armed with the power of Thy Name nothing can ever hurt me, and with Thy love in my heart all the world's afflictions can in no wise alarm me.

Send down, therefore, O my Lord, upon me and upon my loved ones that which will protect us from the mischief of those that have repudiated Thy truth and disbelieved in Thy signs.

Thou art, verily, the All-Glorious, the Most Bountiful.

- Baha'u'llah -

D

Lauded be Thy Name, O Lord my God! I entreat Thee by Thy Name through which the Hour hath struck, and the Resurrection came to pass, and fear and trembling seized all that are in heaven and all that are on earth, to rain down, out of the heaven of Thy mercy and the clouds of Thy tender compassion, what will gladden the hearts of Thy servants, who have turned towards Thee and helped Thy Cause.

Keep safe Thy servants and Thy handmaidens, O my Lord, from the darts of idle fancy and vain imaginings, and give them from the hands of Thy grace a draught of the soft-flowing waters of Thy knowledge.

Thou, truly, art the Almighty, the Most Exalted, the Ever-Forgiving, the Most Generous.

- Baha'u'llah -

E

O my God, ordain this place fortunate and safe. Guard me, O my God, at the moment of my entering and of my leaving it. Ordain it as a fortress to me, and to those who adore Thee and worship Thee, that they may be fortified therein through Thy Favour, and protected therein from the thrusts of the infidels by Thy Power.

Verily, Thou art the Mighty, the Powerful, the Protector, the Honoured, and the Self-Subsistent.

- Baha'u'llah -

F

O God! my God! Shield Thy trusted servants from the evils of self and passion, protect them with the watchful eye of Thy loving-kindness from all rancor, hate and envy, shelter them in the impregnable stronghold of Thy Cause and, safe from the darts of doubtfulness, make them the manifestations of Thy glorious signs. Illumine their faces with the effulgent rays shed from the Dayspring of Thy divine Unity, gladden their hearts with the verses revealed from Thy holy Kingdom, strengthen their loins by Thy all-swaying power that cometh from Thy realm of glory. Thou art the All-Bountiful, the Protector, the Almighty, the Gracious!

- 'Abdu'l-Baha -

G

O my Lord! Thou knowest that the people are encircled with pain and calamities and are environed with hardships and trouble. Every trial doth attack man and every dire adversity doth assail him like unto the assault of a serpent. There is no shelter and asylum for him except under the wing of Thy protection, preservation, guard and custody.

O Thou, the Merciful One! O my Lord! Make Thy protection my armor, Thy preservation my shield, humbleness before the door of Thy oneness my guard, and Thy custody and defense my fortress and my abode. Preserve me from the suggestions of myself and desire, and guard me from every sickness, trial, difficulty and ordeal.

Verily, Thou art the Protector, the Guardian, the Preserver, the Sufficer, and verily, Thou art the Merciful of the Most Merciful!

- 'Abdu'l-Baha -

SEVERANCE

A

Suffer me, O my God, to draw nigh unto Thee, and to abide within the precincts of Thy court, for remoteness from Thee hath well-nigh consumed me. Cause me to rest under the shadow of the wings of Thy grace, for the flame of my separation from Thee hath melted my heart within me. Draw me nearer unto the river that is life indeed, for my soul burneth with thirst in its ceaseless search after Thee. My sighs, O my God, proclaim the bitterness of mine anguish, and the tears I shed attest my love for Thee.

I beseech Thee, by the praise wherewith Thou praisest Thyself and the glory wherewith Thou glorifiest Thine own Essence, to grant that we may be numbered among them that have recognized

Thee and acknowledged Thy sovereignty in Thy days. Help us then to quaff, O my God, from the fingers of mercy the living waters of Thy loving-kindness, that we may utterly forget all else except Thee, and be occupied only with Thy Self. Powerful art Thou to do what Thou willest. No God is there beside Thee, the Mighty, the Help in Peril, the Self-Subsisting.

Glorified be Thy Name, O Thou Who art the King of all Kings!

- Baha'u'llah -

B

Glorified art Thou, O my God! I yield Thee thanks that Thou hast made known unto me Him Who is the Day-Spring of Thy mercy, and the Dawning-Place of Thy grace, and the Repository of Thy Cause. I beseech Thee by Thy Name, through which the faces of them that are nigh unto Thee have turned white, and the hearts of such as are devoted to Thee have winged their flight toward Thee, to grant that I may, at all times and under all conditions, lay hold on Thy Cord, and be rid of all attachment to any one except Thee, and may keep mine eyes directed towards the horizon of Thy Revelation, and may carry out what Thou hast prescribed unto me in Thy Tablets.

Attire, O my Lord, both my inner and outer being with the raiment of Thy favors and Thy loving-kindness. Keep me safe, then, from whatsoever may be abhorrent unto Thee, and graciously assist me and my kindred to obey Thee, and to shun whatsoever may stir up any evil or corrupt desire within me.

Thou, truly, art the Lord of all mankind, and the Possessor of this world and of the next. No God is there save Thee, the All-Knowing, the All-Wise.

- Bahá'u'lláh -

C

Lauded be Thy Name, O my God! I entreat Thee by the fragrances of the Raiment of Thy grace which at Thy bidding and in conformity with Thy desire were diffused throughout the entire creation, and by the Day-Star of Thy will that hath shone brightly, through the power of Thy might and of Thy sovereignty, above the horizon of Thy mercy, to blot out from my heart all idle fancies and vain imaginings, that with all my affections I may turn unto Thee, O Thou Lord of all mankind!

I am Thy servant and the son of Thy servant, O my God! I have laid hold on the handle of Thy grace, and clung to the cord of Thy tender mercy. Ordain for me the good things that are with Thee, and nourish me from the Table Thou didst send down out of the clouds of Thy bounty and the heaven of Thy favor.

Thou, in very truth, art the Lord of the worlds, and the God of all that are in heaven and all that are on earth.

- Baha'u'llah -

D

Many a chilled heart, O my God, hath been set ablaze with the fire of Thy Cause, and many a slumberer hath been wakened by the sweetness of Thy voice. How many are the strangers who have sought shelter beneath the shadow of the tree of Thy oneness, and how numerous the thirsty ones who have panted after the fountain of Thy living waters in Thy days!

Blessed is he that hath set himself towards Thee, and hasted to attain the Day-Spring of the light of

Thy face. Blessed is he who with all his affections hath turned to the Dawning-Place of Thy Revelation and the Fountain-Head of Thine inspiration. Blessed is he that hath expended in Thy path what Thou didst bestow upon him through Thy bounty and favor. Blessed is he who, in his sore longing after Thee, hath cast away all else except Thyself. Blessed is he who hath enjoyed intimate communion with Thee, and rid himself of all attachment to any one save Thee.

I beseech Thee, O my Lord, by Him Who is Thy Name, Who through the power of Thy sovereignty and might, hath risen above the horizon of His prison, to ordain for every one what becometh Thee and beseemeth Thine exaltation.

Thy might, in truth, is equal to all things.

- Bahá'u'lláh -

E

I know not, O my God, what the Fire is which Thou didst kindle in Thy land. Earth can never cloud its splendor, nor water quench its flame. All the peoples of the world are powerless to resist its force. Great is the blessedness of him that hath drawn nigh unto it, and heard its roaring.

Some, O my God, Thou didst, through Thy strengthening grace, enable to approach it, while others Thou didst keep back by reason of what their hands have wrought in Thy days. Whoso hath hasted towards it and attained unto it hath, in his eagerness to gaze on Thy beauty, yielded his life in Thy path, and ascended unto Thee, wholly detached from aught else except Thyself.

I beseech Thee, O my Lord, by this Fire which blazeth and rageth in the world of creation, to rend asunder the veils that have hindered me from appear-ing before the throne of Thy majesty, and from standing at the door of Thy gate. Do Thou ordain for me, O my Lord, every good thing Thou didst send down in Thy Book, and suffer me not to be far removed from the shelter of Thy mercy.

Powerful art Thou to do what pleaseth Thee. Thou art, verily, the All-Powerful, the Most Gener-ous.

- Baha'u'llah -

F

Praise be unto Thee, O my God! I am one of Thy servants, who hath believed on Thee and on Thy signs. Thou seest how I have set myself toward the door of Thy mercy, and turned my face in the direction of Thy loving-kindness. I beseech Thee, by Thy most excellent titles and Thy most exalted attributes, to open to my face the portals of Thy bestowals. Aid me, then, to do that which is good, O Thou Who art the Possessor of all names and attributes!

I am poor, O my Lord, and Thou art the rich. I have set my face toward Thee, and detached myself from all but Thee. Deprive me not, I implore Thee, of the breezes of Thy tender mercy, and withhold not from me what Thou didst ordain for the chosen among Thy servants.

Remove the veil from mine eyes, O my Lord, that I may recognize what Thou hast desired for Thy creatures, and discover, in all the manifestations of Thy handiwork, the revelations of Thine almighty power. Enrapture my soul, O my Lord, with Thy most mighty signs, and draw me out of the depths of my corrupt and evil desires. Write down, then, for me the good of this world and of the world to come. Potent art Thou to do what pleaseth Thee. No God is there but Thee, the All-Glorious, Whose help is sought by all men.

I yield Thee thanks, O my Lord, that Thou hast wakened me from my sleep, and stirred me up, and created in me the desire to perceive what most of Thy servants have failed to apprehend. Make me able, therefore, O my Lord, to behold, for love of Thee and for the sake of Thy pleasure, whatsoever Thou hast desired. Thou art He to the power of Whose might and sovereignty all things testify.

There is none other God but Thee, the Almighty, the Beneficent.

- Bahá'u'lláh -

G

My God! My God! Thou art my Hope and my Beloved, my intended Aim and Desire! With great humbleness and entire devotion I pray to Thee to make me the minaret of Thy love in Thy region, the lamp of Thy knowledge among Thy creatures, and the banner of Thy gift in Thy Kingdom.

Make me one of Thy worshippers who cut themselves from everything but Thee, who sanctify themselves from everything pertaining to the world, and who divert themselves from the defects of the suspicious.

Let my heart be dilated with joy through the spirit of confirmation from Thy Kingdom, and illumine my sight with seeing the hosts of success following one another and descending upon me from Thine Omnipotence.

Thou art Almighty, the Invincible, the Powerful!

- *'Abdu'l-Baha* -

SPIRITUAL QUALITIES

A

Create in me a pure heart, O my God, and renew a tranquil conscience within me, O my Hope! Through the spirit of power confirm Thou me in Thy Cause, O my Best-Beloved, and by the light of Thy glory reveal unto me Thy path, O Thou the Goal of my desire! Through the power of Thy transcendent might lift me up unto the heaven of Thy holiness, O Source of my being, and by the breezes of Thine eternity gladden me, O Thou Who art my God! Let Thine everlasting melodies breathe tranquillity on me, O my Companion, and let the riches of Thine ancient countenance deliver me from all except Thee, O my Master, and let the tidings of the revelation of Thine incorruptible Essence bring me joy, O Thou Who art the most manifest of the manifest and the most hidden of the hidden!

- Baha'u'llah -

B

From the sweet-scented streams of Thine eternity give me to drink, O my God, and of the fruits of the tree of Thy being enable me to taste, O my Hope! From the crystal springs of Thy love suffer me to quaff, O my Glory, and beneath the shadow of Thine everlasting providence let me abide, O my Light! Within the meadows of Thy nearness before Thy presence, make me able to roam, O my Beloved, and at the right hand of the throne of Thy mercy, seat me, O my Desire! From the fragrant breezes of Thy joy let a breath pass over me, O my Goal, and into the heights of the paradise of Thy reality let me gain admission, O my Adored One! To the melodies of the dove of Thy oneness suffer me to hearken, O Resplendent One, and through the spirit of Thy power and Thy might quicken me, O my Provider! In the spirit of Thy love keep me steadfast, O my Succorer, and in the path of Thy good-pleasure set firm my steps, O my Maker!

Within the garden of Thine immortality, before Thy countenance, let me abide for ever, O Thou Who art merciful unto me, and upon the seat of Thy glory stablish me, O Thou Who art my Possessor! To the heaven of Thy loving-kindness lift me up, O my Quickener, and unto the Day-Star of Thy guidance lead me, O Thou my Attractor! Before the revelations of Thine invisible spirit summon me to be present, O Thou Who art my Origin and my Highest Wish, and unto the essence of the fragrance of Thy beauty, which Thou wilt manifest, cause me to return, O Thou Who art my God!

Potent art Thou to do what pleasest Thee. Thou art, verily, the Most Exalted, the All-Glorious, the All-Highest.

- Baha'u'llah -

C

O my Lord! Make Thy beauty to be my food, and Thy presence my drink, and Thy pleasure my hope, and praise of Thee my action, and remembrance of Thee my companion, and the power of Thy sovereignty my succorer, and Thy habitation my home, and my dwelling-place the seat Thou hast sanctified from the limitations imposed upon them who are shut out as by a veil from Thee.

Thou art, verily, the Almighty, the All-Glorious, the Most Powerful.

- Baha'u'llah -

D

O my God, the God of bounty and mercy! Thou art that King by Whose commanding word the whole creation hath been called into being; and Thou art that All-Bountiful One the doings of Whose servants have never hindered Him from showing forth His grace, nor have they frustrated the revelations of His bounty.

Suffer this servant, I beseech Thee, to attain unto that which is the cause of his salvation in every world of Thy worlds. Thou art, verily, the Almighty, the Most Powerful, the All-Knowing, the All-Wise.

- Baha'u'llah -

E

Lauded be Thy Name, O Lord my God! I am Thy servant who hath laid hold on the cord of Thy tender mercies, and clung to the hem of

Thy bounteousness. I entreat Thee by Thy Name whereby Thou hast subjected all created things, both visible and invisible, and through which the breath that is life indeed was wafted over the entire creation, to strengthen me by Thy power which hath encompassed the heavens and the earth, and to guard me from all sickness and tribulation. I bear witness that Thou art the Lord of all names, and the Ordainer of all that may please Thee. There is none other God but Thee, the Almighty, the All-Knowing, the All-Wise.

Do Thou ordain for me, O my Lord, what will profit me in every world of Thy worlds. Supply me, then, with what Thou hast written down for the chosen ones among Thy creatures, whom neither the blame of the blamer, nor the clamor of the infidel, nor the estrangement of such as have withdrawn from Thee, hath deterred from turning towards Thee.

Thou, truly, art the Help in Peril through the power of Thy sovereignty. No God is there save Thee, the Almighty, the Most Powerful.

- Baha'u'llah -

F

O God, refresh and gladden my spirit. Purify my heart. Illumine my powers. I lay all my affairs in Thy hand. Thou art my Guide and my Refuge. I will no longer be sorrowful and grieved, I will be a happy and joyful being. O God, I will no longer be full of anxiety, nor will I let trouble harass me. I will not dwell on the unpleasant things of life.

O God, Thou art more friend to me than I am to myself. I dedicate myself to Thee, O Lord.

- *'Abdu'l-Baha* -

G

O my God! O my God! Glory be unto Thee for that Thou hast confirmed me to the confession of Thy oneness, attracted me unto the word of Thy singleness, enkindled me by the fire of Thy love, and occupied me with Thy mention and the service of Thy friends and maid-servants.

O Lord, help me to be meek and lowly and strengthen me in severing myself from all things and in holding to the hem of the garment of Thy glory, so that my heart may be filled with Thy love and leave no space for the love of the world and the attachment to its qualities.

O God! Sanctify me from all else save Thee, purge me from the dross of sins and transgressions and cause me to possess a spiritual heart and conscience.

Verily thou art merciful and, verily, Thou art the Generous, the Helper!

- 'Abdu'l-Baha -

H

O my Lord! O my Lord! This is a lamp lighted by the fire of Thy love and ablaze with the flame which is ignited in the tree of Thy mercy. O my Lord! Increase his enkindlement, heat and flame, with the fire which is kindled in the Sinai of Thy Manifestation. Verily, Thou art the Confirmer, the Assister, the Powerful, the Generous, the Loving!

- 'Abdu'l-Baha -

I

O my God! O my God! This, Thy servant, hath advanced towards Thee, is passionately wandering in the desert of Thy love, walking in the path of Thy service, anticipating Thy favors, hoping for Thy bounty, relying upon Thy Kingdom, and being exhilarated with the wine of Thy gift, O my God! Increase his fervor in Thy passion, his constancy in Thy praise and his ardor in Thy love. Verily, Thou art the Beneficent and endowed with great bounty! There is no God but Thee, the Forgiving, the Merciful.

- 'Abdu'l-Baha -

J

He is God!

O God, my God! These are servants attracted in Thy days by the fragrances of Thy holiness, enkindled with the flame burning in Thy holy tree, responding to Thy voice, uttering Thy praise, awakened by Thy breeze, stirred by Thy sweet savors, beholding Thy signs, understanding Thy verses, hearkening to Thy words, believing Thy Revelation and assured of Thy loving-kindness. Their eyes, O Lord! are fixed upon Thy Kingdom of effulgent glory and their faces turned toward

Thy dominion on high, their hearts beating with the love of Thy radiant and glorious beauty, their souls consumed with the flame of Thy love, O Lord of this world and the world hereafter, their lives seething with the ardor of their longings for Thee and their tears poured forth for Thy sake.

Shield them within the stronghold of Thy protection and safety, preserve them in Thy watchful care, look upon them with the eyes of Thy providence and mercy, make them the signs of Thy divine unity that are manifest throughout all regions, the standards of Thy might that wave above Thy mansions of grandeur, the shining lamps that burn with the oil of Thy wisdom in the globes of Thy guidance, the birds of the garden of Thy knowledge that warble upon the topmost boughs in Thy sheltering paradise and the leviathans of the ocean of Thy bounty that plunge by Thy supreme mercy in the fathomless deeps.

O Lord, my God! Lowly are these servants of Thine, exalt them in Thy kingdom on high; feeble, strengthen them by Thy supreme power; abased, bestow upon them Thy glory in Thine all-highest realm; poor, enrich them in Thy great dominion. Do

Thou then ordain for them all the good Thou hast destined in Thy worlds, visible and invisible, prosper them in this world below, gladden their hearts with Thine inspiration, O Lord of all beings! Illumine their hearts with Thy joyful tidings diffused from Thine all-glorious Station, make firm their steps in Thy Most Great Covenant and strengthen their loins in Thy firm Testament, by Thy bounty and promised grace, O Gracious and Merciful One! Thou art, verily, the Gracious, the All-Bountiful.

- 'Abdu'l-Baha -

K

He is the Gracious, the All-Bountiful!

O God, my God! Thy call hath attracted me and the Voice of Thy Pen of Glory awakened me. The stream of Thy holy utterance hath enraptured me and the wine of Thine inspiration entranced me. Thou seest me, O Lord! detached from all things but Thee, clinging to the cord of Thy bounty and craving the wonders of Thy grace. I ask Thee, by the eternal billows of Thy loving-kindness and the shining lights of Thy tender care and favor, to grant that which shall draw me nigh unto thee and make me rich in Thy wealth. My tongue, my pen, my whole being, testify to Thy power, Thy might, Thy grace and Thy bounty, that Thou art God and there is none other God but Thee, the Powerful, the Mighty.

I bear witness, at this moment, O my God! to my helplessness and Thy sovereignty, my feebleness and Thy power. I know not that which profiteth me or harmeth me; Thou art verily the All-Knowing, the All-Wise. Do Thou decree for me, O Lord, my God, and my Master, that which will make me feel content with Thine eternal decree and will prosper me in every world of Thine. Thou art in truth the Gracious, the Bountiful.

Lord! Turn me not away from the ocean of Thy wealth and the heaven of Thy mercy, and ordain for me the good of this world and hereafter. Verily, Thou art the Lord of the mercyseat, enthroned in the highest; there is none other God but Thee, the One, the All-Knowing, the All-Wise.

- 'Abdu'l-Baha -

L

He is the prayer-hearing, prayer-answering God!

By Thy glory, O Beloved One, Thou giver

of light to the world! the flames of separation have consumed me and my waywardness hath melted my heart within me. I ask of Thee, by Thy Most Great Name, O Thou the Desire of the world and the Well-Beloved of mankind! to grant that the breeze of Thine inspiration may sustain my soul, that Thy wondrous voice may reach my ear, that my eyes may behold Thy signs and Thy light as revealed in the manifestations of Thy names and Thine attributes, O Thou within Whose grasp are all things!

Thou seest, O Lord, my God, the tears of Thy favored ones, shed because of their separation from Thee and the fears of Thy devoted ones in their remoteness from Thy Holy Court. By Thy power, that swayeth all things, visible and invisible! It behooveth Thy loved ones to shed tears of blood for that which hath befallen the faithful at the hands of the wicked and the oppressors on the earth. Thou beholdest, O my God! how the ungodly have compassed Thy cities and Thy realms! I ask Thee by Thy Messengers and Thy chosen Ones and by Him whereby the standard of Thy divine unity hath been implanted amidst Thy servants, to shield them by Thy bounty. Thou art, verily, the Gracious, the All-Bountiful.

And, again, I ask Thee by the sweet showers of Thy grace and the billows of the ocean of Thy favor, to ordain for Thy saints that which shall solace their eyes and comfort their hearts. Lord! Thou seest him that kneeleth yearning to arise and serve Thee, the dead calling for eternal life from the ocean of Thy favor and craving to soar to the heavens of Thy wealth, the stranger longing for his home of glory 'neath the canopy of Thy grace, the seeker hastening by Thy mercy to Thy door of bounty, the sinful turning to the ocean of forgiveness and pardon.

By Thy sovereignty, O Thou Who art glorified in the hearts of men, I have turned to Thee, forsaking mine own will and desire, that Thy holy will and pleasure may rule within me and direct me according to that which the pen of Thy eternal decree hath destined for me. This servant, O Lord, though helpless turneth to the Orb of Thy power, though abased hasteneth unto the Day-Spring of glory, though needy craveth the ocean of Thy grace. I beseech Thee by Thy favor and bounty, cast him not away. Thou art verily the Almighty, the Pardoner, the Compassionate.

- 'Abdu'l-Baha -

STEADFASTNESS

A

Glorified be Thy Name, O Lord my God! I beseech Thee by Thy power that hath encompassed all created things, and by Thy Sovereignty that hath transcended the entire creation, and by Thy Word which was hidden in Thy wisdom and whereby Thou didst create Thy heaven and Thy earth, both to enable us to be steadfast in our love for Thee and in our obedience to Thy pleasure, and to fix our gaze upon Thy face, and celebrate Thy glory. Empower us, then, O my God, to spread abroad Thy signs among Thy creatures, and to guard Thy Faith in Thy realm. Thou hast ever existed independently of the mention of any of Thy creatures, and wilt remain as Thou hast been for ever and ever.

In Thee I have placed my whole confidence, unto Thee I have turned my face, to the cord of Thy loving providence I have clung, and toward the shadow of Thy mercy I have hastened. Cast me not as one disappointed out of Thy door, O my God, and withhold not from me Thy grace, for Thee alone do I seek. No God is there beside Thee, the Ever-Forgiving, the Most Bountiful.

Praise be to Thee, O Thou Who art the Beloved of them that have known thee!

- Baha'u'llah -

B

O Thou Whose nearness is my wish, Whose presence is my hope, Whose remembrance is my desire, Whose court of glory is my goal, Whose abode is my aim, Whose Name is my healing, Whose love is the radiance of my heart, Whose service is my highest aspiration! I beseech Thee by Thy Name, through which Thou hast enabled them that have recognized Thee to soar to the sublimest heights of the knowledge of Thee and empowered such as devoutly worship Thee to ascend into the precincts of the court of Thy holy favors, to aid me to turn my face toward Thy face, to fix mine eyes upon Thee, and to speak of Thy glory.

I am the one, O my Lord, who hath forgotten all else but Thee, and turned toward the Dayspring of Thy grace, who hath forsaken all save Thyself in the hope of drawing nigh unto Thy court. Behold me, then, with mine eyes lifted up toward the Seat that shineth with the splendors of the light of Thy Face. Send down, then, upon me, O my Beloved, that which will enable me to be steadfast in Thy Cause, so that the doubts of the infidels may not hinder me from turning toward Thee.

Thou art, verily, the God of Power, the Help in Peril, the All-Glorious, the Almighty.

- Baha'u'llah -

C

Glorified art Thou, O Lord my God! I beseech Thee by Him Who is Thy Most Great Name, Who hath been sorely afflicted by such of Thy creatures as have repudiated Thy truth, and Who hath been hemmed in by sorrows which no tongue can describe, to grant that I may remember Thee and celebrate Thy praise, in these days when all have turned away from Thy beauty, have disputed with Thee, and turned away disdainfully from Him Who is the Revealer of Thy Cause. None is there, O my Lord, to help Thee except Thine own Self, and no power to succor Thee save Thine own power.

I entreat Thee to enable me to cleave steadfastly to Thy Love and Thy remembrance. This is, verily, within my power, and Thou art the One that knoweth all that is in me. Thou, in truth, art knowing, apprised of all. Deprive me not, O my Lord, of the splendors of the light of Thy face, whose brightness hath illuminated the whole world. No God is there beside Thee, the Most Powerful, the All-Glorious, the Ever-Forgiving.

- Bahá'u'lláh -

D

O Lord, my God! Assist Thy loved ones to be firm in Thy Faith, to walk in Thy ways, to be stead-fast in Thy Cause. Give them Thy grace to withstand the onslaught of self and passion, to follow the light of Divine Guidance. Thou art the Powerful, the Gracious, the Self-Subsisting, the Bestower, the Compassionate, the Almighty, the All-Bountiful.

- 'Abdu'l-Baha -

E

Make firm our steps, O Lord! in Thy path and strengthen Thou our hearts in Thine obedience. Turn our faces toward the beauty of Thy oneness, and gladden our bosoms with the signs of Thy divine unity. Adorn our bodies with the robe of Thy bounty, and remove from our eyes the veil of sinfulness and give us the chalice of Thy grace; that the essence of all beings may sing Thy praise before the vision of Thy grandeur. Reveal then Thyself, O Lord! by Thy merciful utterance and the mystery of Thy Divine Being, that the holy ecstasy of prayer may fill our souls--a prayer that shall rise above words and letters and transcend the murmur of syllables and sounds--that all things may be merged into nothingness before the revelation of Thy splendor.

Lord! These are servants that have remained fast and firm in Thy Covenant and Thy Testament, that have held fast unto the cord of constancy in Thy Cause and clung unto the hem of the robe of Thy grandeur. Assist them, O Lord! with Thy grace, confirm with Thy power and strengthen their loins in obedience to Thee.

Thou art the Pardoner, the Gracious.

- 'Abdu'l-Baha -

F

O God, my God! I have turned in repentance unto Thee, and verily Thou art the Pardoner, the Compassionate.

O God, my God! I have returned to Thee, and verily Thou art the Ever-Forgiving, the Gracious.

O God, my God! I have clung to the cord of Thy bounty, and with Thee is the storehouse of all that is in heaven and earth.

O God, my God! I have hastened toward Thee, and verily Thou art the Forgiver, the Lord of grace abounding.

O God, my God! I thirst for the celestial wine of Thy grace, and verily Thou art the Giver, the Bountiful, the Gracious, the Almighty.

O God, my God! I testify that Thou hast revealed Thy Cause, fulfilled Thy promise and sent down from the heaven of Thy grace that which hath drawn unto Thee the hearts of Thy favored ones. Well is it with him that hath held fast unto Thy firm Cord and clung to the hem of Thy resplendent Robe!

I ask Thee, O Lord of all being and King of the seen and unseen, by Thy power, Thy majesty and Thy sovereignty, to grant that my name may be recorded by Thy pen of glory among Thy devoted ones, them whom the scrolls of the sinful hindered not from turning to the light of Thy countenance, O prayer-hearing, prayer-answering God!

- 'Abdu'l-Baha -

G

O Compassionate God! Thanks be to Thee for Thou hast awakened and made me conscious. Thou hast given me a seeing eye and favored me with a hearing ear; hast led me to Thy Kingdom and guided me to Thy Path. Thou hast shown me the right way and caused me to enter the Ark of Deliverance. O God! Keep me steadfast and make me firm and staunch. Protect me from violent tests and preserve and shelter me in the strongly fortified fortress of Thy Covenant and Testament. Thou art the Powerful! Thou art the Seeing! Thou art the Hearing! O Thou the Compassionate God! Bestow upon me a heart which, like unto glass, may be illumined with the light of Thy love, and confer upon me a thought which may change this world into a rose-garden through the spiritual bounty. Thou art the Compassionate, the Merciful! Thou art the Great Beneficent God!

- *'Abdu'l-Baha* -

TEACHING

A

Praise be to Thee, O Lord my God! I implore Thee, by Thy Name which none hath befittingly recognized, and whose import no soul hath fathomed; I beseech Thee, by Him Who is the Fountain-Head of Thy Revelation and the Day-Spring of Thy signs, to make my heart to be a receptacle of Thy love and of remembrance of Thee. Knit it, then, to Thy most great Ocean, that from it may flow out the living waters of Thy wisdom and the crystal streams of Thy glorification and praise.

The limbs of my body testify to Thy unity, and the hair of my head declareth the power of Thy sovereignty and might. I have stood at the door of Thy grace with utter self-effacement and complete abnegation, and clung to the hem of Thy bounty, and fixed mine eyes upon the horizon of Thy gifts.

Do Thou destine for me, O my God, what becometh the greatness of Thy majesty, and assist me, by Thy strengthening grace, so to teach Thy Cause that the dead may speed out of their sepulchers, and rush forth toward Thee, trusting wholly in Thee, and fixing their gaze upon the orient of Thy Cause, and the dawning-place of Thy Revelation.

Thou, verily, art the Most Powerful, the Most High, the All-Knowing, the All-Wise.

- Bahá'u'lláh -

B

Glory be unto Thee, O Thou God of the world and desire of the nations, O Thou Who hast become manifest in the Greatest Name, whereby the pearls of wisdom and utterance have appeared from the shells of the great sea of Thy knowledge, and the heavens of religions are adorned with the light of the appearance of the sun of Thy countenance!

I beg of Thee--by that Word, by reason of which Thy proof was made perfect among Thy creatures and Thine argument among Thy servants--to strengthen Thy people in that whereby the face of the Cause will radiate in Thy dominion and the standards of Thy power and the banners of Thy guidance will be planted in Thy lands and among Thy servants!

O my God! Thou beholdest them clinging to the robe of Thy grace and holding fast unto the hem of the mantle of Thy beneficence. Ordain for them that which may draw them nearer unto Thee, and withhold them from all else save Thee.

I beg of Thee, O Thou King of existence and protector of the seen and unseen, to make whosoever arises to serve Thy Cause as a sea moving by Thy desire; ablaze with the fire of Thy Sadrat, shining from the horizon of the heaven of Thy will. Verily, Thou art the mighty One, Whom neither the power of all the world, nor the strength of nations can weaken. There is no God but Thee, the One, the Single, the Protector, the Self-Subsistent.

- Baha'u'llah -

C

O God, Who art the Author of all Manifestations, the Source of all Sources, the Fountain-Head of all Revelations, and the Well-Spring of all Lights! I testify that by Thy Name the heaven of understanding hath been adorned, and the ocean of utterance hath surged, and the dispensations of Thy providence have been promulgated unto the followers of all religions.

I beseech Thee so to enrich me as to dispense with all save Thee, and be made independent of any one except Thyself. Rain down, then, upon me out of the clouds of Thy bounty that which shall profit me in every world of Thy worlds. Assist me, then, through Thy strengthening grace, so to serve Thy Cause amidst Thy servants that I may show forth what will cause me to be remembered as long as Thine own Kingdom endureth and Thy dominion will last.

This is Thy servant, O my Lord, who with his whole being hath turned unto the horizon of Thy bounty, and the ocean of Thy grace, and the heaven of Thy gifts. Do with me then as becometh Thy majesty, and Thy glory, and Thy bounteousness, and Thy grace.

Thou, in truth, art the God of strength and power, Who art meet to answer them that pray Thee. There is no God save Thee, the All-Knowing, the All-Wise.

- Baha'u'llah -

D

O Lord! Open Thou the door. Provide the means, prepare the way, make safe the path. That we may be guided to those souls, whose hearts are prepared for Thy Cause, and that they may be guided to us. Verily, Thou art the Merciful, the Most Bountiful, the All-Powerful.

- 'Abdu'l-Baha -

E

O my Glorious Lord! Help me to refrain from every irregular inclination; to subdue every rebellious passion; to purify the motives of my conduct; to conform myself to that meekness which no provocation can ruffle; to that patience which no affliction can overwhelm; to that integrity which no self-interest can shake; that I may be qualified to serve Thee and to teach Thy Word.

- 'Abdu'l-Baha -

TESTS AND DIFFICULTIES

A

Dispel my grief by Thy bounty and Thy generosity, O God, my God, and banish mine anguish through Thy sovereignty and Thy might. Thou seest me, O my God, with my face set toward Thee at a time when sorrows have compassed me on every side. I implore Thee, O Thou Who art the Lord of all being, and overshadowest all things visible and invisible, by Thy Name whereby Thou hast subdued the hearts and the souls of men, and by the billows of the Ocean of Thy mercy and the splendors of the Day-Star of Thy bounty, to number me with them whom nothing whatsoever hath deterred from setting their faces toward Thee, O Thou Lord of all names and Maker of the heavens.

Thou beholdest, O my Lord, the things which have befallen me in Thy days. I entreat Thee, by Him who is the Day-Spring of Thy names and the Dawning-Place of Thine attributes, to ordain for me what will enable me to arise to serve Thee and to extol Thy virtues. Thou art, verily, the Almighty, the Most Powerful, Who art wont to answer the prayers of all men!

And, finally, I beg of Thee by the light of Thy countenance to bless my affairs, and redeem my debts, and satisfy my needs. Thou art He to Whose power and to Whose dominion every tongue hath testified, and Whose majesty and Whose sovereignty every understanding heart hath acknowledged. No God is there but Thee, Who hearest and art ready to answer.

- Baha'u'llah -

B

Lauded and glorified art Thou, O my God! I entreat Thee by the sighing of Thy lovers and by the tears shed by them that long to behold Thee, not to withhold from me Thy tender mercies in Thy Day, nor to deprive me of the melodies of the Dove that extolleth Thy oneness before the light that shineth from Thy face. I am the one who is in misery, O God! Behold me cleaving fast to Thy Name, the All-Possessing. I am the one who is sure to perish; behold me clinging to Thy Name, the Imperishable. I implore Thee, therefore, by Thy Self, the Exalted, the Most High, not to abandon me unto mine own self and unto the desires of a corrupt inclination. Hold Thou my hand with the hand of Thy power, and deliver me from the depths of my fancies and idle imaginings, and cleanse me of all that is abhorrent unto Thee.

Cause me, then, to turn wholly unto Thee, to put my whole trust in Thee, to seek Thee as my Refuge, and to flee unto Thy face. Thou art, verily, He Who, through the power of His might, doeth whatsoever He desireth, and commandeth, through the potency of His will, whatsoever He chooseth. None can withstand the operation of Thy decree; none can divert the course of Thine appointment. Thou art, in truth, the Almighty, the All-Glorious, the Most Bountiful

- Baha'u'llah -

C

O Thou Whose tests are a healing medicine to such as are nigh unto Thee, Whose sword is the ardent desire of all them that love Thee, Whose dart is the dearest wish of those hearts that yearn after Thee, Whose decree is the sole hope of them that have recognized Thy truth! I implore Thee, by Thy divine sweetness and by the splendors of the glory of Thy face, to send down upon us from Thy retreats on high that which will enable us to draw nigh unto Thee. Set, then, our feet firm, O my God, in Thy Cause, and enlighten our hearts with the effulgence of Thy knowledge, and illumine our breasts with the brightness of Thy names.

- Baha'u'llah -

D

Glory be Thee, O my God! But for the tribula tions which are sustained in Thy path, how could Thy true lovers be recognized; and were it not for the trials which are borne for love of Thee, how could the station of such as yearn for Thee be revealed? Thy might beareth me witness! The companions of all who adore Thee are the tears they shed, and the comforters of such as seek Thee are the groans they utter, and the food of them who haste to meet Thee is the fragments of their broken hearts.

How sweet to my taste is the bitterness of death suffered in Thy path, and how precious in my estimation are the shafts of Thine enemies when encountered for the sake of the exaltation of Thy word! Let me quaff in Thy Cause, O my God, whatsoever Thou didst desire, and send down upon me in Thy love all Thou didst ordain. By Thy glory! I wish only what Thou wishest, and cherish what Thou cherishest. In Thee have I, at all times, placed my whole trust and confidence.

Raise up, I implore Thee, O my God, as helpers to this Revelation such as shall be counted worthy of Thy Name and of Thy sovereignty, that they may remember me among Thy creatures, and hoist the ensigns of Thy victory in Thy land.

Potent art Thou to do what pleaseth Thee. No God is there but Thee, the Help in Peril, the Self-Subsisting.

- Baha'u'llah -

E

Glorified art Thou, O Lord my God! Every man of insight confesseth Thy sovereignty and Thy dominion, and every discerning eye perceiveth the greatness of Thy majesty and the compelling power of Thy might. The winds of tests are powerless to hold back them that enjoy near access to Thee from setting their faces towards the horizon of Thy glory, and the tempests of trials must fail to draw away and hinder such as are wholly devoted to Thy will from approaching Thy court.

Methinks, the lamp of Thy love is burning in their hearts, and the light of Thy tenderness is lit within their breasts. Adversities are incapable of estranging them from Thy Cause, and the vicissitudes of fortune can never cause them to stray from Thy pleasure.

I beseech Thee, O my God, by them and by the sighs which their hearts utter in their separation from Thee, to keep them safe from the mischief of Thine adversaries, and to nourish their souls with what Thou hast ordained for Thy loved ones on whom shall come no fear and who shall not be put to grief.

- Baha'u'llah -

F

Is there any Remover of difficulties save God? Say: Praised be God! He is God! All are His servants, and all abide by His bidding!

- *The Bab* -

G

Say: God sufficeth all things above all things, and nothing in the heavens or in the earth but God sufficeth. Verily, He is in Himself the Knower, the Sustainer, the Omnipotent.

- *The Bab* -

H

He is the Compassionate, the All-Bountiful! O God, my God! Thou seest me, Thou knowest me; Thou art my Haven and my Refuge. None have I sought nor any will I seek save Thee, no path have I trodden nor any will I tread but the path of Thy love. In the darksome night of despair, my eye turneth expectant and full of hope to the morn of Thy boundless favor and at the hour of dawn my drooping soul is refreshed and strengthened in remembrance of Thy beauty and perfection.

He whom the grace of Thy mercy aideth, though he be but a drop, shall become the boundless ocean, and the merest atom which the outpouring of Thy loving-kindness assisteth, shall shine even as the radiant star.

Shelter under Thy protection, O Thou Spirit of purity, Thou Who art the All-Bountiful Provider, this enthralled, enkindled servant of Thine. Aid him in this world of being to remain steadfast and firm in Thy love and grant that this broken-winged bird attain a refuge and shelter in Thy Divine Nest, that abideth upon the Celestial Tree.

- 'Abdu'l-Baha -

I

O Lord, my God and my Haven in my distress! My Shield and my Shelter in my woes! My Asylum and Refuge in time of need and in my loneliness my Companion! In my anguish my Solace, and in my solitude a loving Friend! The Remover of the pangs of my sorrows and the Pardoner of my sins!

Wholly unto Thee do I turn, fervently imploring Thee with all my heart, my mind and my tongue, to shield me from all that runs counter to Thy will in this, the cycle of Thy divine unity, and to cleanse me of all defilement that will hinder me from seeking, stainless and unsullied, the shade of the Tree of Thy grace.

Have mercy, O Lord, on the feeble, make whole the sick, and quench the burning thirst.

Gladden the bosom wherein the fire of Thy love doth smolder and set it aglow with the flame of Thy celestial love and spirit.

Robe the tabernacles of divine unity with the vesture of holiness and set upon my head the crown of Thy favor.

Illumine my face with the radiance of the Orb of Thy bounty and graciously aid me in ministering at Thy Holy Threshold.

Make my heart overflow with love for Thy creatures and grant that I may become the sign of Thy mercy, the token of Thy grace, the promoter of concord amongst Thy loved ones, devoted unto Thee, uttering Thy commemoration and forgetful of self but ever mindful of what is Thine.

O God! My God! Stay not from me the gentle gales of Thy pardon and grace, and deprive me not of the well-springs of Thine aid and favor.

'Neath the shade of Thy protecting wings let me nestle, and cast upon me the glance of Thine all-protecting eye.

Loose my tongue to laud Thy Name amidst Thy people, that my voice may be raised in great assemblies, and from my lips may stream the flood of Thy praise.

Thou art, in all truth, the Gracious, the Glorified, the Mighty, the Omnipotent.

- 'Abdu'l-Baha -

J

O my Lord, my Beloved, my Desire! Befriend me in my loneliness and accompany me in my exile; remove my sorrow, cause me to be devoted to Thy Beauty, withdraw me from all else save Thee, attract me through Thy fragrances of holiness, cause me to be associated in Thy Kingdom with those who are severed from all else save Thee, and who long to serve Thy sacred threshold and who stand to work in Thy Cause. Enable me to be one of Thy maid-servants who have attained to Thy good pleasure. Verily, Thou art the Gracious, the Generous!

- 'Abdu'l-Baha -

TIMES OF TROUBLE

A

"O thou who art turning thy face towards God! Close thine eyes to all things else, and open them to the realm of the All-Glorious. Ask whatsoever thou wishest of Him alone; seek whatsoever thou seekest from Him alone. With a look He granteth a hundred thousand hopes, with a glance He healeth a hundred thousand incurable ills, with a glimpse He layeth balm on every wound, with a nod He freeth the hearts from the shackles of grief. He doeth as He doeth, and what recourse have we? He carrieth out His Will, He ordaineth what He pleaseth. Then better for thee to bow down thy head in submission, and put thy trust in the All-Merciful Lord."

- 'Abdu'l-Baha -

To be used at midnight followed by the recitation of the Greatest Name "Ya Allah El-Mustaghath" which means: "O God Our Deliverer, whom we Invoke in times of extreme need, danger, or crisis!"

O My God! I beg Thee by the King of Names and Maker of heaven and earth, by the rustling of the leaves of the Tree of Life, and by the Utterances through which the realities of things are drawn unto us, to grant me __________ *[here name your supplications, wish, or needs].*

Then repeat 95 times: Ya Allah El-Mustaghath!

- Baha'u'llah -

B

Glory is Thine, O my God, and praise is to Thee, O my Lord! I ask Thee, by Thy Name which manifests Thy power and Thy strength, to purify the mirrors of the hearts of Thy servants from the dross of doubt and uncertainty, and to lead the wandering souls to Thy light, so that they may realize Thy Oneness and acknowledge Thy

Singleness. O my God! There is no refuge save Thee, and there is no pathway but leads to Thine abode. When Thy people learn of Thee, O God, they will not leave Thy way. Help them to remain constant and faithful while on this journey to Thee, so that they may reach Thy Kingdom and attain Thy will. Thou art the Almighty, the Merciful.

- Baha'u'llah -

C

O God! Assist me with the hosts of the Supreme Concourse and make me firm and steadfast in the Covenant and Testament. I am weak in the Covenant and the Testament, confer upon me strength; I am poor, bestow upon me wealth from the treasury of the Kingdom; I am ignorant, open before my face the doors of knowledge; I am dead, breathe into me the breath of life; I am dumb, grant me an eloquent tongue so that with a fluent expression I may raise the call of thy Kingdom and guide all to the firmness of thy Covenant. Thou art the Generous, the Giver, and the Mighty!

- 'Abdu'l-Baha -

UNITY

A

O my God! O my God! Unite the hearts of Thy servants, and reveal to them Thy great purpose. May they follow Thy commandments and abide in Thy law. Help them, O God, in their endeavor, and grant them strength to serve Thee. O God! leave them not to themselves, but guide their steps by the light of Thy knowledge, and cheer their hearts by Thy love. Verily, Thou art their Helper and their Lord.

- Baha'u'llah -

B

O my God! O my God! Verily, I invoke Thee and supplicate before Thy threshold asking Thee that all Thy mercies may descend upon these souls.

Specialize them for Thy favor and Thy truth. O Lord! Unite and bind together the hearts, join in accord all the souls and exhilarate the spirits through the signs of Thy sanctity and oneness. O Lord! Make these faces radiant through the light of Thy oneness. Strengthen the loins of Thy servants in the service of Thy kingdom. O Lord, Thou possessor of infinite mercy! O Lord of forgiveness and pardon! Forgive our sins, pardon our shortcomings and cause us to turn to the kingdom of Thy clemency, invoking the kingdom of might and power, humble at Thy shrine and submissive before the glory of Thine evidences. O Lord God! Make us as waves of the sea, as flowers of the garden, united, agreed through the bounties of Thy love. O Lord! Dilate the breasts through the signs of Thy oneness and make all mankind as stars shining from the same height of glory, as perfect fruits growing upon Thy Tree of Life. Verily, Thou art the Almighty, the Self-Subsistent, the Giver, the Forgiving, the Pardoner, the Omniscient, the One Creator!

- 'Abdu'l-Baha -

DYNAMICS OF PRAYER FOR SOLVING PROBLEMS

FIVE STEPS FOR SOLVING A PROBLEM OF ANY KIND

"O Thou Whose Tests are a healing Medicine to such as are nigh unto Thee..."

These following five steps were suggested by Shoghi Effendi based upon a Tablet of Baha'u'llah regarding meditative decision and contemplation with God to ACT through the **Dynamic Power of Prayer.** This timeless thought--a means of finding solutions through the use of prayer--speaks to us all about the dynamics of prayer, the power of turning inwardly to the spiritual Reality of God, and how we can use this to find solutions to even our most challenging problems. Entering into deep inward prayerful communion with God; meditating upon the problem; remaining in sustained silent contemplation; allowing the solution to present itself; fixing upon the decision, implementing the decision in real life action are all explicit aspects as given by Baha'u'llah in his *Tablet of the Dynamic Power of Prayer*.

According to 'Abdu'l-Baha:

> *"We should speak in the language of heaven -- in the language of the spirit -- for there is a language of the spirit and heart. It is as different from our language as our own language is different from that of the animals, who express themselves only by cries and sounds. It is the language of the spirit which speaks to God. When, in prayer, we are freed from all outward things and turn to God, then it is as if in our hearts we hear the voice of God. Without words we speak, we communicate, we converse with God and hear*

the answer. ... All of us, when we attain to a truly spiritual condition, can hear the Voice of God."

"We must strive to attain to that condition by being separated from all things and from the people of the world and by turning to God alone. It will take some effort on the part of man to attain to that condition but he must work for it, strive for it. We can attain to it by thinking and caring less for material things and more for the spiritual. The further we go from the one, the nearer we are to the other--the choice is ours! Our spiritual perception, our inward sight must be opened so that we can see the signs and traces of God's spirit in everything. Everything can reflect to us the light of the spirit."

Following these five steps, is the specific prayer with instructions from Baha'u'llah's Tablet--though any prayer may be used in this format.

THE FIVE STEPS as given by Shoghi Effendi:

First Step: Pray and meditate about it. Use the prayers of the Manifestations as they have the greatest power. Then remain in the silence of contemplation for a few minutes.

Second Step: Arrive at a decision and hold this. This decision is usually born during the contemplation. It may seem almost impossible of accomplishment but if it seems to be an answer to a prayer or a way of solving the problem, then immediately take the next step.

Third Step: Have determination to carry the decision through. Many fail here. The decision, budding into determination, is blighted and instead becomes a wish or a vague longing. When determination is born, immediately take the next step.

Fourth Step: Have faith and confidence that the power will flow through you, the right way will appear, the door will open, the right thought, the right message, the right principle, or the right book will be given to you. Have confidence and the right thing will come to your need. Then, as you rise from prayer, take at once the fifth step.

Fifth Step: Then, lastly, ACT. Act as though it had all been answered. Then act with tireless, ceaseless energy. And as you act, you, yourself, will become a magnet, which will attract more power to your being, until you become an unobstructed channel for the Divine power to flow through you.

Many pray but do not remain for the last half of the first step. Some who meditate arrive at a decision, but fail to hold it. Few have the determination to carry the decision through, still fewer have the confidence that the right thing will come to their need. But how many remember to act as though it had all been answered? How true are these words 'Greater than the prayer is the spirit in which it is uttered' and greater than the way it is uttered is the spirit in which it is carried out.

Tablet of the Dynamic Power of Prayer

In regard to his DECISION to ACT, let him repeat nineteen times:

O my God! Thou seest me severed completely from all things save Thee! Clinging to none other but Thee! I fervently implore Thee, O Lord!--to GUIDE me in all my doings and perilous endeavors toward that which shall profiteth me in Thy Cause and glorify my manners, purify my attitude, and confirm my behaviors and those of the loftiness of the exalted stations of all Thy servants and Thy loved ones seeking the perfection of their true selves.

Let him then reflect upon the matter and take ACTION upon whatsoever cometh to mind. The stubborn opposition of the adversaries will then indeed give way to the The Most Prosperous Supremacy.

- Baha'u'llah -

"Perish that lover who discerneth between the pleasant and the poisonous in his love for his Beloved!"

- Baha'u'llah -

"O thou who hast been sore afflicted on the pathway of the Covenant! Anguish and torment, when suffered on the pathway of the Lord, Him of manifest signs, is only favour and grace; affliction is but mercy, and grief a gift from God. Poison is sugar on the tongue, and wrath is kindness, nourishing the soul. Then praise thou Him, the loving Provider, for having ordained this dire affliction, which is but bounty unalloyed."

- 'Abdu'l-Baha -

If I, like Abraham, through flames must go,
Or yet like John a bloodstained road must run;
If, Joseph-like, Thou'd cast me in a well,
Or shut me up within a prison cell--
Or make me e'en as poor as Mary's Son--
I will not go from Thee,
But ever stand
My soul and body bowed to Thy command.

- 'Abdu'l-Baha -

FROM THE AQDAS

Recite ye the verses of God every morn and eventide. Whoso faileth to recite them hath not been faithful to the Covenant of God and His Testament, and whoso turneth away from these holy verses in this Day is of those who throughout eternity have turned away from God. Fear ye God, O My servants, one and all. Pride not yourselves on much reading of the verses or on a multitude of pious acts by night and day; for were a man to read **a single verse with joy and radiance** it would be better for him than to read with lassitude all the Holy Books of God, the Help in Peril, the Self-Subsisting. Read ye the sacred verses in such measure that ye be not overcome by languor and despondency. Lay not upon your souls that which will weary them and weigh them down, but rather what **will lighten and uplift them**, so that they may soar on the wings of the Divine verses towards the Dawning-place of His manifest signs; this will draw you nearer to God, did ye but comprehend.

God hath enjoined upon you to observe the utmost cleanliness, to the extent of washing what is soiled with dust, let alone with hardened dirt and similar defilement. Fear Him, and be of those who are pure. Should the garb of anyone be visibly sullied, his prayers shall not ascend to God, and the celestial Concourse will turn away from him.

- Baha'u'llah -

"YA ALLAH EL-MUSTAGHATH!"

"Oh God Our Deliverer, whom we invoke in times of extreme need, danger, or crisis!"

To be prayed or repeated 1000 times between midnight and dawn for 9 or 19 nights (though to use the prayer once daily or even 9 or 19 times is enough). It seems infallible, even marvelous in power. 'Abdu'l-Baha said it for 3 days just before WWI ended.

"Ya Allah El-Mustaghath!--'Oh God Our Deliverer, whom we invoke in times of extreme need, danger, or crisis!'" Shoghi Effendi (*en route* to university in England) said to Madame Ali Kuli Khan, when on a visit to Barbizon, in the forest of Fontainebleau, "I give you this! It is a free translation, as he translated it at her request."

'Abdu'l-Baha, when in America, related to Khan and several of the friends, that at the end of two years of his Father's absence in Sulaymaniyyih he had been praying fervently for His return, to quiet the unrest which activities of Subh-i Azal were causing the friends in Baghdad. One night he had prayed this one prayer all night when, at dawn there came a knocking at the gate and a messenger arrived from the Prince of Nur, announcing His return. The Master went forth to welcome Him with some of the friends. Soon after Baha'u'llah declared His Manifestation.

In Persia, the friends of His Holiness the Bab used to pray this prayer, repeating it one thousand times, between midnight and dawn, for the protection or for whatever they desired. They might in those days, it is said, leave in the morning and be killed before return at night. They believed this prayer had a very special potency and often it was answered before 9 days had passed.

In Paris, when Shoghi Effendi was on his way to the university in England, he told Madame Kahn that shortly before World War I ended, he used to accompany 'Abdu'l-Baha to Haifa, and each week they would spend four days usually looking after the shrines and to see about conditions in general. One day the Master closed his door and Shoghi Effendi (he said) knelt outside it, leaning his head against it. For eight continuous hours the Master paced to and fro in the room, praying only one prayer: "YA ALLAH EL-MUSTAGHATH!"

When Shoghi Effendi related this to Madame Ali Kuli-Khan she exclaimed "Why it was shortly after this that the European War ended!" Shoghi Effendi smiled, but did not reply either yes or no.

In 1924, when she was leaving the presence of the Guardian at Haifa, en-route for Persia to America, she enquired if there were any prayers she could use for special help.

The Guardian smiled and replied: "Is there any prayer better than "Ya Allah El-Mustaghath?" showing he recalled their conversation in Paris. This was the prayer repeated over and over by the Master, as he paced his garden when the Turkish ship was coming to take him away.

'Abdu'l-Baha in one Tablet states that "Ya Allah El-Mustaghath" is to be repeated 95 times and, in another Tablet, 81 times. Letters from Shoghi Effendi, as well as other prayers, clarify that repetition is a matter of individual choice. In a postscript added in his own handwriting to a letter to an individual, Shoghi Effendi states: "There is no objection to saying "Ya Allah El-Mustaghath" any time you like and as often as you like." (Notes taken by Mme. Khan, February 23, 1938)

Blessed is the spot, and the house,
and the place, and the city,
and the heart, and the mountain,
and the refuge, and the cave,
and the valley, and the land,
and the sea, and the island,
and the meadow where mention
of God hath been made,
and His praise glorified.

- Baha'u'llah -

16384553R00079

Printed in Great Britain
by Amazon